Home Based Business Opportunities

14 <u>GREAT</u> Home Based Business Ideas for everyone.

Casimir Biriyok

"The past cannot be changed.
The future is yet in your power."

- Unknown

British Library Cataloguing in Publication Data

A catalogue record for this book is available from the British Library.

ISBN: 978-1-9161463-0-3   (paperback)

ISBN: 978-1-9161463-1-0   (ebook)

First Published in 2019 by Biriyok Publishing Ltd,

 Kemp House, 160 City Road, London EC1V 2SN.

www.biriyokpublishing.com

info@biriyokpublishing.com

Biriyok Publishing Ltd
the future in your hands

Registered Office

Biriyok Publishing Ltd, Kemp House, 160 City Road, London EC1V 2SN.

Typeset for Biriyok Publishing Ltd

Printed in Great Britain for Bririyok Publishing Ltd by:

CMP (UK) Ltd, Poole, Dorset,

Biriyok Publishing Publishes books in a variety of print and electronic formats and also print on demand (pod). Some materials included in the e books may not be included the print version vice versa.

LEGAL DISCLAIMERS

The Information presented herein represents the view of the Author. The author and publisher have made every effort to ensure that the information in this book was correct at date of publication. The author and publisher do not assume and hereby disclaim any liability to any party for any loss, damage, or disruption caused by errors or omissions, whether such errors or omissions result from negligence, accident, or any other cause. Change is the only constant; as such the author's right to update views based on new development is reserved.

Under no circumstances will any legal responsibility or blame be held against the Author or the publisher for any reparation, damages or monetary loss due to the information herein, either directly or indirectly.

Any perceived slights against anybody or organisations are unintentional. The author makes no representation of warranty with respect to this book specifically disclaims any implied warranties or merchantability of fitness for any particular purpose and shall in no event be liable for any loss of profit or any commercial damage , including but not limited to special , incidental, consequential, or other damages.

The publisher has used its best endeavours to ensure that the websites addresses referred to in this book are correct and active at the time of going to press. However, the publisher and the author have no responsibility for the websites and cannot make guarantee that a site will remain live or that the content will remain relevant, decent or appropriate,

FTC Affiliate Disclaimer Statements

Some of the links in the e book or paperback edition may be affiliate links and if you go through them to make a purchase we may earn a commission. Keep in mind that I link these companies and their products because of their quality and not because of the commission I receive from your purchases. The decision is yours, and whether or not you decide to buy something is completely up to you.

DEDICATION

This book is dedicated to those who want a better tomorrow by taking action today. It is especially for those who believe that distance and cost are no barriers to quality knowledge for a better tomorrow. Also for my family who think I am great no matter what.

CONTENTS

INTRODUCTION

The Daily Nightmare

"Ideas are worthless. Execution is what matters."

– Dane Carlson

Two hours. This is how long the average daily commute in the USA, Canada or United Kingdom is. If one works for five days a week, this amounts to 40 hours a month. This is the time that one could use for resting, relaxing, doing something productive in the house or spending quality time with family. The daily commute is no joyride either, no thanks to commuters who play their music rather too loudly, put their feet up on the seats, and talk noisily into their phones.

Transport costs are not making it any easier, nor the fact that some workers have become "extreme commuters" travelling for up to four hours to and from work, because relocating nearer to the workplace is next to impossible.

For some, the daily commute has become a steady and enduring nightmare, something they cannot wake up from. So they grit their teeth and soldier on. They need to get to the workplace, come hell or high water.

Working from Home

In the past, there was no escaping the daily commute. If you did not get to work, you could not put food on the table. Fortunately, today's workers have a choice: home-based work. Thanks to the internet. There now exists many ways to earn, even without leaving the comforts of home.

Working from home does not just free you from the horrors of commuting, it also gives you more time to spend with your family, allows you to save on transportation costs, daily allowances and taxes, and offers you more freedom to do the things that you love, without sacrificing your income. Furthermore, working from home can help you build your wealth, something you might not be able to do with just a regular 9-5 job. No wonder more and more people are joining the work from home bandwagon. It is easy enough to get a-work-from-home job; if you are not very picky and have the skills required for the job you can do some data entry work, build apps, write articles, or work as a virtual assistant and or online marketer. Some people who are not quite ready to give up their day jobs take on part time online tasks for the extra cash. Others take on full-time stints that pay well. And then there are those who have given up their 9-5 workdays so they can build and grow their own businesses.

Are You Cut for the Home Based Business?

Becoming one's own boss is perhaps the biggest attraction working from home offers. Imagine calling the shots and not having to answer to anyone but yourself. But before you throw caution to the wind and hand your boss your immediate resignation, make sure that this is something you really want to do. Otherwise, you are setting yourself up for failure. Here are some questions you must answer as truthfully as possible:

1. **Are you disciplined and committed enough?** Building your own business requires more than just a desire to free yourself from the confines of your office cubicle. It takes commitment and perseverance. Contrary to what some people believe, home based businesses demand hard work. Being an entrepreneur is not easy, and it will not make you rich immediately.

2. **Are you a self-starter?** If you want to be your own boss and have your own business, then you must make sure that you can get the job done. You will be building your own business, so you have only yourself to depend on. You will have to motivate, inspire and push yourself, because nobody else will. You must also be comfortable working alone; unlike in the office, you most likely will have no one to turn on to for suggestions, ideas or help.

3. **Can you manage your time properly?** Home-based businesses require not just discipline, perseverance and commitment: they also demand time. If you want to be a home-based business owner, you must have excellent time management skills. You must have strategies in place for accomplishing everything your home-based business needs without sacrificing time that you could use in pursuing other worthwhile activities, like spending it with your family.

If you answer yes to these three questions, then a home based business just might be for you. No matter who or what you are – a corporate manager who is tired of the daily grind, an employee who wants to have more freedom, an individual who wants to create streams of income that will generate more money or a stay-at-home parent who wants to augment the family income, you can become a successful home based business owner if you have the smarts and the right attitude.

"What business should I start?" Is, of course, the first question all aspiring home-based business owners must ask themselves, and that is where this book comes in. In the next chapters you will learn 14 home-based business ideas that you could try your hand at. Each chapter discusses one business idea, the steps you must take in launching the business and how you can market the idea to reach your potential customers. The last chapter features links and resources that you could refer to for pointers, insights and inspiration.

Make yourself comfortable and read your way to starting your own home-based business. Should you find your courage and your resolve faltering, take wisdom from **Zig Ziglar: "You don't have to be great to start, but you have to start to be great."**

CHAPTER 1.

IDEA 1 – Creating Information Based Products to Sell

"Ideas can be life-changing. Sometimes all you need to open the door is just one more good idea."

– Jim Rohn

Faced with the question "What kind of business should I start?" Many people fall into the default thinking that the best business involves something that sells fast, for example, food, clothing, and probably unique and quirky items, for a profit. These people are right; you want profit, so you need something to sell. But while food and the other aforementioned items do sell, you would need some capital in order to sell them. But what exactly, do you do when you do not have the capital? You sell information instead.

Information is one of the greatest commodities in the world for the simple reason that everyone needs it. Information mobilizes the world; it helps people go through daily life, do their jobs and pursue their passions.

Fortunately, information is available to almost anyone, provided by experts and people who possess great chunks of knowledge about different things. Of course, no one holds the information to everything, and so experts in one field will refer to those who specialize in other areas. You know something the next person does not, in the same way that they have information on things unfamiliar to you.

Information can be found anywhere; from the people in your home, in your neighborhood, in schools; and thanks to the internet, you can even find information on a small gadget that fits snugly in your jeans pocket.

And because information is a very important commodity, anyone can make a profit from sharing it. Ever wondered why being a teacher, a trainer, a consultant or a coach never goes out of style or why there can never be enough books or websites? Because all these services provide information.

Information sells. When done right, it provides you a source of income you probably did not even think you could make. Selling information, therefore, is a business that is here to stay. One can never go wrong in choosing to sell information, which explains why many have taken the road to selling information-based products.

Example Ideas

These products come in many forms: e-books, web content, audiobooks, webinars, video courses, computer software, smartphone applications and similar merchandise. Information-based products also include live workshops, coaching and mentoring sessions and membership sites. People buy not just songs or movies; they also check the Internet for information they need. They visit different websites not just for entertainment but also for learning. They google their health symptoms; they look for recipes; they watch video tutorials.

If you know a great deal about something, you can turn your knowledge into a moneymaking undertaking. You can start a blog or make online videos that can earn for you through online advertising. Better yet, you can write e-books on the subject and earn passive income. Since writing e-books will entail the same amount of time and effort, regardless of the copies you sell, it is a good way to earn income. The only thing you need to invest is your time and effort in writing the e-book.

But what if you are not an expert on anything? Do not be too quick to shelve this business idea. According to Kyle Eschenroeder of startupbros. com you can create an information-based product even if you know nothing about the subject by following these tips:

- Mix and match information from different sources. If you do not know a single thing about the subject you want to make an information product on, then source the information from different websites, books, videos and people. Most of the information on the internet is free for the taking. It is up to you, how you would use all that free information. You can find a new spin and bring even old (but not out-dated) information into a new form that people would want to pay to get a hold of. But why would people want to pay for something they can get without cost? Because people are busy or simply lazy. Instead of going through all the results in their internet search, people interested in raising chickens would rather buy an e-book that compiles all of the important information they need. Of course, you need to give credit to the sites you got your information from.

- **Channel experts.** Let us say that you have been playing with the idea of creating an e-book on home schooling, since the number of home-schooled kids in the UK and rest of the World is rising. You have no children and no experience whatsoever in home schooling, so how are you going to do this? By interviewing experts. If you think this is a rather ambitious activity, think again. Teachers, parents of home schoolers, researchers and authors will be more than happy to oblige you, because you are helping them spread their ideas. You do not even have to step out of your house to do the interview. You can set up a web conference, record it and sell the video afterwards. You can also take existing audio and video interviews, transcribe them and sell them in e-book format.

- **Go the PLR route.** There are many Private Label Rights (PLR) e-books and audiobooks available for various purposes. You buy a bundle of the same topic, tweak, modify or combine the information they contain and ta-da! You have a brand new e-book or audiobook to sell for a profit. You can even translate the content into another language so you can have a brand spanking new information product.

- **Gather popular questions and answer them.** Come up with a questionnaire for your target audience. If you are targeting novice novel writers, set up a one-page site and then ask them what their biggest issues and frustrations are. Once you have gathered the most common questions, compile them and research the answers. Write the answers in an easily digestible form and you have an e-book to sell. You can also make an audiobook from the answers, which you can sell for a higher price.

- **Outsource writing talent.** The above mentioned tips are inspirations enough for anyone who can string words together to make a coherent e-book; but what if you do not have the knack for writing? You can hire someone who can put together your e-book for you. You can go to Craigslist.com, Upwork.com, PeoplePerHour.com or similar outsourcing websites to get a freelancer to write that e-book. If you can get someone to write a

10 thousand word e-book for $200 (approximately £150), you will only need to sell 20 copies of your $10 e-book to break even. If you have a good marketing strategy, your e-book will continue to sell for a long time.

Getting Started

Selling information-based products is guaranteed to be lucrative business, but only if you know exactly what you are doing. The first thing you have to do is to decide on a subject or niche. What kind of information do you want to sell? If you are highly passionate about something, say, playing the ukulele, then you can consider making the instrument the subject of your information-based product. However, your interest or expertise should not be the sole basis for your decision, especially because your aim is to gain profit. You must also look into market demand, or how many people are looking for the kind of information you have about the ukulele.

The Google Adwords Keyword Planner Tool, which comes with a Google Adwords account, is one such tool you can use to assess market demand. This tool provides information on the amount of online searches for a specific keyword or phrase made through Google per month. Although a high volume of searching does not necessarily translate to a high demand for a certain product, it is a good place to start. You must also look at related searches and examine how some of the higher volume specific searches pertain to your original keyword. For example, if you are searching for "smallholding," you might want to look at the related searches like "smallholding business ideas" or "small holding for sale Yorkshire or New York." You then reference these keywords or phrases with your original keyword in order to determine more accurately whether there is a high demand for your idea. Later on you might also want to use paid tools in order to get more specific items and statistics about market demand.

After looking at the market demand, you would also want to look at the competition. The bigger the competition is the less chances you have of having a lot of people buy your information product. To check the competition, you can go to Amazon and search for your keyword and its related results. From there you will see how many competitors there are for your product idea or keyword. From there you can decide to narrow your niche in a way that would allow you to address high demand with the least competition as possible.

Taking the Idea to Market

The following is a suggested step-by-step process you can study, tweak and apply to create your information product. Of course, your first attempt at creating a product and selling it will be difficult, but it will get better overtime.

1. **Determine your market.** Who would buy your information product? You must understand your target market so you can tailor the content of your information product for them. Knowing your target audience is critical in adapting your approach or presentation, the language and the format you would use, plus the examples you would include in your information product.

2. **Write the text.** This is, of course, the most critical step in the process. Needless to say, the information you present must be of great value to your audience; otherwise, you will not see the results that you expect. The best way to start is by identifying a sore spot, a problem or an issue that your target audience has about the subject. If your subject is about financial freedom, you can visit blogs and forums dedicated to financial freedom and pick up ideas and insights. Shape your text around the major insight or issue. Be thorough and make sure to come up with practical solutions to the problem in clear language that is easy to understand.

   Think of a specific title that would draw potential readers in: instead of giving your e-book the rather boring title "The Path to Financial Freedom," you could call it "How to Become Financially Free in 365 Days or Less."

   Choose a simple and consistent font throughout and limit your styles, headers and colour schemes to a minimum. This is to ensure readability of the e-book. Proofread the text for style, grammar and spelling errors.

Very important: If writing is not your forte, outsource some writing talent from Upwork.com or other similar sites, as mentioned previously. Be detailed with your instructions, and if possible, include some of the research you have made so the writer can include the information you have in the text. It is also important to have a professional proofread the work for you to ensure that there are no errors in the construction of the e-book.

3. **Get an attractive cover for your e-book.** A well-designed cover will help your e-book look professional and worth buying. You can refer to existing e-books for cover ideas. You can choose to design your own cover using your own artwork or photos. You can never go wrong with hiring someone to design the cover for you.

4. **Convert the text into different file formats.** You can convert your e-book into a PDF file, which is supported by all e-readers. However, some e-readers like the Amazon Kindle, does not always render PDFs in good shape, so it is best to make your e-book available in all formats: .pdf, .mobi for the Amazon Kindle and .epub for the Barnes & Noble Nook, the Apple iBookstore, Kobo and most other e-readers. If you have knowledge of CSS, HTML and Epub design, you can opt to do the conversion yourself. You can also use the services offered by e-book publishers such as sigil-ebook.com, smashwords.com or kdp.amazon.com or hire someone to convert the text for you.

   Similarly, you can record yourself or someone else reading the text and then sell the work as an audiobook - something that author, speaker and entrepreneur Joanna Penn has done. You can also outsource and have someone else do the recording for you.

5. **Write your sales page.** The sales page is a standalone page created for the sole purpose of selling your information product. Written well, this page can convert mere visitors into becoming your customers. Therefore, your sales page must be striking and persuasive.

6. **Upload your e-book to your website with the e-commerce tool of your choice, like** founderu.selz.com **or** gumroad.com**.** You can also make use of e-publishing services like kdp.amazon.com, pubit.barnesandnoble.com, .kobo.com/writinglife or any similar websites, like those listed herein. Should you self-publish or make use of e-publishing services? Get insights from alexisgrant.com or post by janefriedman.com

Marketing the Idea

After your information product has been made, you need to market it in order for people to know about it. Even if you have made the best ever e-book or audiobook, you cannot get people to buy it if you do not make noise. Here are some of the ways you can make your product known:

1. **Through Facebook marketing.** Almost everyone is on Facebook, so it is a great way of getting the word out. Here are some of the most effective ways of using Facebook to reach your target audience:

   • **Facebook business page.** If you already have a Facebook account, you can set up a business page, which you can leverage by publishing relevant and attractive content, photos and videos.

     Through the business page, you can also interact with your target audience and followers to keep them engaged. Be careful not to overdo promoting your product. Although product promotion is your main aim, you do not want to fill your followers' feeds with posts about your e-book, because this might cause them to unfollow your page. Instead, engage them with relevant and entertaining content.

   • **Facebook ads.** Facebook offers different kinds of ads that suit different needs, such as directing users to your Facebook business page or website, promoting your product or targeting audiences. Like any other ad, Facebook ads are offered at different costs, so it pays to know what kind of ad you would want and how much you would be willing to pay. wordstream. com offers some technical information you need to know about

Facebook ads, including cost. adespresso.com provides a definitive guide on Facebook Advertising.

- **Facebook groups.** This is another way of driving customer engagement. Create an exclusive group, invite your followers and build a community. Using Facebook groups, you can build relationships, promote events and even give rewards to your members. A group would also allow you to get feedback for new ideas or products. While Facebook groups are free, they require a lot of work and maintenance in order to increase engagement.

2. **Through Google AdWords.** Google AdWords is an advertising service that allows your website to show up in the results on a SERP (search engine results page). Websites organically rank high in a SERP through having good content, but this takes time. With Google AdWords, you do not have to wait for your website to show up in a SERP. By using paid search, you can ensure that your ad appears either on the top or the side of the SERP. This way, you will get more traffic to your site, which can result in increased sales. Bestselling author, marketer and entrepreneur Neil Patel offers a detailed guide to understanding how AdWords works and how you can set up your first ad campaign.

3. **Through affiliate marketing.** Affiliate marketing is a system wherein you can get other people to promote your information product in their respective websites. In return, these people – your affiliates – earn a commission for every sale you make through their recommendation. Supposing you are selling an e-book about DIY projects. You sign up through an affiliate network like ClickBank. ClickBank introduces your website and product to its many member affiliates, whom you have to woo, to make sure that they promote your website. You will also find a detailed explanation about how you can recruit affiliates to draw traffic to your site and increase your sales at www.clickbank.com

4. **Through rich, relevant, useful and attractive content.** Content will help you gain a following. You cannot just create an information product, market it through the above-mentioned

channels and hope that people will buy it. You must first have a website (or a blog at the very least) which you can create free with Wix.com or Wordpress.com. Your website must have content that will draw people in and push them to get even more visitors for you. If you are not a natural writer, you can hire someone to do the writing for you. You must also build your email list, which you can do by offering first-time visitors to your site a freebie in exchange for their email address. This freebie could be free advice, a video tutorial or anything that your audience would find value in. You can then use this email list to send updates to keep your followers engaged.

5. **Through various social media networks.** You want to get the word out about your information product, so you must use as many channels as you can: your personal Facebook page, Twitter, Instagram, Snapchat, YouTube and other similar networks. Of course, your choice of social media to use depends on the demographic of your target market. Again, you need to come up with share-worthy and engaging content to keep the Internet a-buzz with your website and product.

CHAPTER 2:

IDEA 2 – Selling Products Through Affiliation

Affiliate marketing has made businesses millions and ordinary people millionaires.

-Bo Bennet

Selling products through affiliation is one of the simplest home-based businesses model there is. It does not require expertise, and can be done at your own pace. While the affiliate online business has the potential of earning up to $5000 a month, it is not safe to go full throttle into selling through affiliation if you have not learned the ropes yet. For starters, you can turn to affiliate marketing as an income generator on the side while you continue your day job or manage your other online businesses. Test the waters first, and see if it works for you.

If this idea does not appeal to you because selling is not really your cup of tea or coffee, worry not. You do not need to call people or knock on people's doors, because selling as an affiliate does not require you to do cold calling or hard selling. What you need, instead, is a lot of patience and hard work. Although it is simple enough, you will need to put in a lot of work in order to make this business idea work for you. Affiliate marketing is not as easy as some marketers would make it seem.

In the previous section, you have been given an idea of how affiliate marketing works. Basically, you get people to click on a link that will take them to a merchant's product page. When a customer buys the product through the link you provided, then you get a cut or a commission from what the merchant earns through that sale.

Affiliate Marketing in a Nutshell

How exactly do you get people to buy something that you talk about or recommend? By producing content that is engaging enough to make people want to get the product you are supporting. To do this, you must have your own website. Building a custom website can take weeks (and money of course, especially if you are hiring someone to set the site up), but you can set up a site free of charge through Wordpress.com, Wix.com, Web.com and other free website builders. One thing you must note about free websites is hosting. In order for your site to be found on the Internet, it needs to be hosted on a web server, much like a brick and mortar store needs to have an exact location. There are many free web hosting sites, but it is always advisable to have a paid hosting account which is reliable, secure and does not have bandwidth limitations, unlike free hosting. Paid hosting sites like www.bluehost.com/track/nclwebhosting and http://inmotion-hosting.evyy.net/c/1499603/260033/4222 are good and have used both.

Once you have a website, the next thing you need to do is to look for products that you feel a strong affinity for. You write content about the products you like, spread the word through various methods, and get people to buy these products through the links you provide with your content. When the merchant makes a sale, you get a commission: a percentage from the profits the merchant gets.

Example Ideas

The kind of products (or services) to promote depends on where your interests lie. Generally, you should gravitate towards products or services that you personally use. If you want to really attract people toward a certain merchandise or brand, you must be willing and able to vouch for it. You cannot just bluff and hope that people will believe you and buy the product. Having used the product yourself, you should personally know both its good and bad points. This will help you write more realistic and trustworthy reviews. Today's audiences are smart and savvy, so they will be quick to spot whether a certain write-up is honest or not. The more credible you are, the greater the likelihood of people buying through your affiliate links.

That said, you should choose products that can be trusted. Of course, you will want to choose a product that has a lot of potential. To do this, you must spend a considerable amount of time doing research. As much as possible, go for trusted and distinguished brands; not only are they well-known, but more often than not, their products are also of a higher quality than less popular brands.

Of course, you want this business (even if it is only a side business at first) to last, so promote evergreen products as much as possible. Evergreen products are those that are always in demand. They are products that people will keep buying, long after they have been introduced to the market.

Examples of good products to get affiliate income from include:

- **Dating, love and relationship products.** People will always be looking for someone special to love, so dating apps and relationship advice would be in high demand.
- **Parenting**. According to UNICEF, around 350,000 children are born each day. As long as children are being born, there will be parents who need parenting products, especially information-based products that deal with every aspect of parenting. And because parenting is a rather broad subject, there are a lot of products to try and promote from baby essentials to child discipline, schooling and a lot more.
- **Weight loss products**. E-books, workout regimens, apps that target weight loss and diet plans are just some of the ideas under this category. Being fit never goes out of style, and people will always be looking for products and services that can help them reach their ideal weight.
- **Body and muscle building products**. People will not stop at weight loss. When they reach their ideal weight, people will be so enthusiastic from their success that they will continue on to muscle building. In the past, only the male demographic was the focus of this kind of product, but females have also started gaining muscle as part of their fitness efforts. Protein supplements, gym subscriptions, meal plans and other related products are very popular nowadays, and will undoubtedly stay in demand for many years.
- **Self-help products.** This kind of product is in demand, not just because of the increased number of people afflicted with depression and anxiety, but also because of the stress that comes with living day to day. People are always on the lookout for ways to improve not just their daily situation, but their mind-set as well; so information products, online courses, health supplements and relaxation essentials are hot commodities.

These are just some of the many products you can sell as an affiliate. By doing your research, you can find the perfect product that interests you and will give you an opportunity to boost your existing income.

It goes without saying that you will only achieve success as an affiliate marketer if you do it right. Therefore, take note of the following three mistakes that most newbie affiliate marketers face. Be sure to avoid these and you will have a greater chance of earning quickly.

1. **Promoting products just for the heck of it.** Yes, the main idea of having an affiliate marketing business is to earn commissions, but that does not mean you will promote any product just because it will earn you money. In order to get a lot of clicks and affiliate sales, you need to drive traffic to your website or blog. You can only do this if you have content that is attractive and engaging. If you promote just anything, you will probably lose your readership especially when your audience realizes that you are just there to make money out of their clicks and purchases. You must establish a relationship with your readers, and the sales (and commission) will follow.

2. **Promoting products that are of no value to your audience.** If you have chosen the parenting niche, then the products and services you promote must all be about parenting. There is no sense including links that pertain to life coaching or financial freedom, no matter how good the product is. What you can do, instead, is to create different streams in your website so each stream can have a different audience according to the niche.

3. **Promoting too many or too few products.** If you have too many links and ads on your website, you will drive away your page visitors. No one wants to read through ad after ad. Instead, focus on making your website valuable to your visitors by interspersing links of your promoted products throughout the site. On the other hand, promoting too few products will not really help you achieve your goal of earning from your links. The key is finding the balance between these two extremes. As a beginner, you will have difficulty at first, but as you go on learning about affiliate marketing and producing note-worthy content and interacting with your audience, you will eventually find this balance.

Getting Started

Before going into the affiliate marketing business, make sure that you are thoroughly decided upon setting this business up. Like any other business, affiliate marketing takes commitment. It is easy to get discouraged at first, especially if you are just starting out. But if you commit yourself to the task and do everything right, you will make a good profit from selling products as an affiliate.

If you are really sure you are in for the long haul, then you can begin setting up your business by deciding on the niche. Again, niche refers to a subset of the market that is focused on specific needs. In plain-speaking, a niche is a narrower target market. Say, if you are thinking about yoga, you might want to narrow the niche down to yoga for weight loss, which is more specific.

While you do not want to dwell on a subject that is too broad, you also do not want to settle for too narrow a topic because a very small audience might not translate to the sales you aim for.

Once you have decided on the niche, you can build your website or a blog at the very least. Start posting content and attracting visitors with your posts while searching for good products to promote and increasing your knowledge about affiliate marketing. Again, know that you will not be able to have visitors to your site unless you use marketing tactics, which will be outlined later on.

Of course, in order to reach your audience, you must get right down to the very heart of your target audience and know exactly what they want and need. You can do this by holding surveys or polls, asking them questions and interacting with them through your blog, or through Facebook and other social media sites.

You would also do well to look at other websites in the same niche as your choice. Which products are they promoting? What kind of tactics do they use? How often do they post updates on their site or blog? Are they well-known in social media circles? Asking these questions does not make you sneaky; it makes you well-informed. By looking at how others are able to create success, you can follow suit.

Taking the Idea to Market

Once you have figured out your niche and what your target audience needs, start looking for good products to promote by signing up with an affiliate network such as clickbank.com, which happens to be the one of the oldest affiliate marketplaces in existence. You might also want to research on other affiliate networks.

For the purposes of illustration, let us look at how you can do a search on ClickBank:

Sign in and click the "Marketplace" tab. On the left side of the page, you will see the different categories of available products. Choose the category that fits your niche. You can even make it narrower by clicking on a subcategory.

After clicking on the category or subcategory, you will see the following numbers or metrics. These are the numbers that you need to look at in order to determine which products you want to promote:

- **Initial $/sale**. This refers to the amount that you, as an affiliate, will earn each time the product gets sold through your affiliate link.
- **Avg $/sale**. This is the average amount you can make for every sale. Most newbies make the mistake of choosing the product with the highest avg $/sale, but this is not always correct. You might get a big commission selling a high-priced diet plan, but you might get only two or three buyers (also called conversions). It would be better to go with a lower-priced product for which you can successfully get many conversions.
- **Avg %/sale**. This is the average commission rate you earn from all the sales of a merchant's product.
- **Grav**. This refers to gravity, or the representation of how many affiliates were able to make a sale of the product in the last 12 weeks. More recent transactions are given a higher value, so the higher the gravity, the more in demand the product is. However, a high gravity number can also mean that there is a lot of competition, so you might not be earning as much as you expect.

- **Avg Rebill Total**. This refers to the amount you can make on all rebilled sales, that is, products that have recurring billing, like subscriptions or memberships that customers have to pay regularly.
- **Avg % Rebill**. This is the commission rate you can earn from the rebills.

You should also look at the sales page or landing page of the product. The more "organic" and helpful it looks and feels the better. So after looking at all these numbers, you will want to choose products that have a low cost, an engaging sales page and gravity above 20. Of course, it is up to you to decide on the product, but try to choose one that will get you the most number of buyers or conversions.

Once you have decided on the product, click the red PROMOTE button. A pop-up window will open asking you to input a Tracking ID. It is best to input a unique ID or link for the different channels you use for promoting the product, so you know where the sale is coming from. For example, if you are promoting the product through email, maybe you can put in an ID like product-email1 or if you are sharing the link through Facebook, you can create an ID that says product-fb.

Providing Value for Your Target Audience

After you have found the product to promote, it is time to start writing content focused on the product. Again, engaging content is very important; this will build trust in your audience and make them want to buy what you are promoting. Too often, affiliate marketers only use certain ways to put the affiliate link out there, such as:

- **Reviews.** Everyone who wants to buy something would like to read reviews about the product they are meaning to buy. By writing a review that shows the product's good points without being biased, an affiliate marketer can ensure continuous sales.
- **Banners.** Some marketers just look for a blog post or article that is somehow related to the product and affix a banner somewhere in the page, hoping that someone will be interested enough to click on it and buy the product. While simple enough to do, banners hardly ever result in a sale.

- **Content links.** Other marketers will relate a story or a situation and intersperse their article or blog post with links leading to the product's sale page. If the reader likes it, then he will probably buy the product. This is a good way of directing a reader to the product, but only if the content is written properly and does not read like it is promoting the product at all. This would also work for a marketer who has a reputation for being a trustworthy authority on the niche.

You can do all these, but you can be a better affiliate by following the system suggested by AuthorityHacker.com. In a nutshell, the system goes like this:

1. You write an engaging article or blog post that touches on the niche, but you do not mention the product at all. What the readers will see is an article that is helpful for them. You do not want to show them upfront that you are promoting some product because they will probably not read your article when they know that you are merely trying to sell them something.
2. You share the article on social media or through ads. When people click on the link you posted on Facebook or another social media site, they are brought to the article. On the same page, they will see an offer – a free e-book maybe, or special advice that they can get in exchange for their email address.
3. Using the email list you have gathered from those who opted in for the freebie, you send updates that slowly hook them into your subject. You then send them a link to your "thank you and offer page," which now talks about how they could benefit from buying the product. Of course, this offer page contains the affiliate link to the product. When they are sold to the idea that the product can give them huge benefits, they will go to the sales page and buy the product, and you get your commission.

Marketing the Idea

Again, the key to marketing your affiliate links is through great content. By writing powerfully engaging and interesting blogs, you can gain the readership of your target audience. If you provide value through your articles and posts, you will also gain the trust of your audience. The better your reputation is, the higher the chance of people buying the products that you recommend.

Blogging and content writing is one way of spreading your affiliate links, but you can also do so through Facebook marketing. You can set up a business page on Facebook, run ads on the social media site or form a Facebook group that allows you to touch base with your followers regularly.

You can also use Google AdWords to help your blog or website show up in the SERP, therefore increasing the chances of people going to your site and buying the products you promote.

CHAPTER 3:

IDEA 3 – Creating Online Training Courses

"We need to bring learning to people instead of people to learning."

- Elliot Masie

Online training courses are one of the hottest products on the Internet today, all thanks to a population that is ever-hungry for information. Online learning also presents the following advantages over traditional classroom learning:

1. **Less time-consuming.** One can learn knowledge and skills online just by logging in to a learning portal. There is no need to get dressed or to drive or compute to the physical campus. Plus, since online courses are focused on teaching specific skills, there is no need to learn things that are not really related to your subject of study, which makes the time for learning even shorter.

2. **More savings.** Of course, online courses are cheaper than tuition for traditional schools. Traditional degrees cost 80% more than online courses.

3. **More flexibility.** Online courses allow anyone to learn, such as, full-time parents, those with full-time jobs, college dropouts. Anyone who wants to learn a certain skill can do so just by signing up, paying and taking a course online. They can choose to do so at their convenience, without having to disrupt their normal everyday schedule.

4. **A more focused skill set.** Online courses zero in on specific skills. Therefore, one can learn more in less time. This translates to better chances of you getting a job based on those skills.

It is not surprising, then, that there are more and more people taking online courses. And because there is a large market for online courses, creating online courses is a lucrative business idea you might want to try your hand at.

Is Creating Online Training Courses for You?

Anyone who has considerable knowledge about something can create an online course, much like anyone can make an information-based product. If you are unsure about what to teach (as most newbie course creators are), then you can start by looking at your interests. What are you passionate about? This question should replace what is the first question you might be asking yourself: "What do you know?" If you think and feel that there is nothing that you could teach anyone.

But the good thing about not knowing about a topic is that you can learn about it, and that while learning, you can teach others. All you need is your laptop, a camera, a microphone, a screen recording and editing software and an e-learning platform. Before we go on to discuss the steps you must take, let us look at the different kinds of courses you can come up with.

Example Ideas

Online training courses take many forms. They run the entire gamut from online law degrees to how-to tutorials. They can be as short as 30 minutes or as long as three hours. They can be about physics, politics, cryptography or designing your website. The topics for online courses are diverse, but if there is one thing in common that these courses share, it is that they all sell.

What kind of course would you make, if you could? Ideally, of course, you would want to make a course which would earn you a large amount. If you were an engineer, a doctor, a lawyer or a teacher you could be trusted to create an online course that people would find helpful. And since you are an established expert, you can expect people to pay for the courses you produce, even at a high price.

But what if you are not really an expert? What if you are just the average Jane or Joe? Would you still be able to profit from a business such as this? The short answer is yes. Of course, you have to work in order to produce courses that people will actually want to buy. If you cannot think of a topic to feature in your course, here are some ideas you might want to consider:

- How to achieve Internet fame
- Navigating through various social media networks
- How to write an information-based product
- Affiliate marketing 101
- Preparing baby meals weekly
- How to lose weight in 90 days
- Healthy school lunches
- How to start a home-based online business

These are just some of the many ideas that can inspire your own first attempt at making an online training course. Ultimately, you want to create a course on something that you are familiar with and interested in. The more you know about the subject, the more confident you will be about creating it and the better your final product will be.

Taking the Idea to Market

Ready to launch your home-based online training course creation? Here are some steps you can follow:

1. **Know your audience.** Once you have decided on the topic of your course, you can start drafting the course content. Of course, you want to give information that your potential customers will find valuable. As such, it pays to know your target audience. Who are your target customers? What exactly would they want to learn about the subject of your choice? What will they get from taking the course you will offer? You need to think like your audience so you can determine whether the course you are creating will be worth paying for or not.

   In order to find out what your potential customers want and need, you have to do your research. Go to forums that talk about your target subject and find out what problems or issues there are that you can give solutions to. If you already have a following from your blog or website, you can ask your readers for their difficulties and challenges. Doing so will give you the direction you need in writing the course. You can also visit blogs about the same niche and subject so you could get ideas about what your target customers need.

   It would also do you good to look at the kind of information products or online courses the competition offers and use what you have learned as a springboard into how you will approach the making of the course.

2. **Form your idea about the course.** After identifying a problem that your target audience has, gather information and materials by doing research. This is very important, especially if you are not an expert in your chosen subject or topic. What you can do is

gather as much information as you can and organize it in such a way that it will be easy for your target audience to digest. Should you find a lot of competition on the subject, then you can use the best information from the competition to make your course really valuable.

Think of how you can make the course unique and a cut above the rest. Maybe you can provide a freebie, like a mini-course, that will not only help your target market but also entice them to buy the full course.

If possible, plan the course in smaller, easier-to-digest chunks that will make writing it and presenting it easier. In addition, your target customers will be much more receptive to shorter courses that promise clear outcomes at the end.

3. **Write the course.** Use clear and easy to understand language. Remember that your aim is not to impress, but to make your customers learn something – whether it is a skill or a way to make something. Be guided by the expected outcomes of the course as you write. Remember to include only essential information. While related ideas might be helpful, be careful not to muddle the course with information your target learners do not really need.

   As much as possible, use more than one medium. While reading text works for a lot of people, including photos, video and audio can ensure further absorption of concepts.

4. **Decide on the format of your course.** How do you want to present your course? You can use a screen-capturing recorder like Camtasia, if your course is about teaching someone how to do something on your computer screen. Or you can make it look as if you are the teacher and record yourself while you are explaining the concepts with a whiteboard and a marker.

   You can use PowerPoint or a PDF for showing the text and the graphics that accompany it. You can also use other applications and software that you are familiar with.

5. **Create the course.** After planning and writing the course and deciding the format that you will use, it is time to put the course together. Pay careful attention to the structure of the course and how you will deliver it.

It is natural for you to feel inadequate or have issues about how you look on camera, or how your voice sounds on the microphone. But cut yourself some slack. This is your first time, after all. As you get used to producing courses, you will find that it gets easier and the quality of your courses gets better. However, make sure that you do not give out mediocre information. Again, you want to sell your course, so be sure that everything in it will be of value to your customers.

6. **Decide on where you will upload your course.** If you have a website and already have a huge following, you can use your website and your mailing list to promote the course and sell it to your readers and followers. The beauty about selling your courses yourself is that you get to keep all the earnings and profits to yourself. You can also create a special page for your course subscribers that can provide them even more value – special tips and tricks, a forum where the learners can discuss with you and their peers, or even some personal email support from you.

You can also opt to upload your course in Udemy.com or other online academies such as biriyok.com, Mlearningsite.com and other similar learning platforms. The beauty of using an online learning platform is that you do not have to promote the courses yourself. These platforms have their own traffic and their own followers, so you can earn something even if you are too lazy to promote your online course. This is also the reason beginners like you would do well to launch their first courses in learning platforms. Once you get the hang of putting courses together and you have made a name for yourself in the niche, then you can probably start selling your courses on your own site.

Learning platforms also allow learners to review courses, which is beneficial for you, but only if your course is put together well. Naturally, you need to produce a high quality course, even if it is as simple as cross-stitching. Of course, you need to create prompts for your learners to leave reviews and their takeaways from the course, especially if they have enjoyed it. Reviews are important so other learners who are looking for courses will be encouraged and inspired to take the course too. To get your learners to leave reviews, you can also give them incentives, like a course upgrade or a special video clip that will further enhance the knowledge or skill they have gained from the course.

Once the course is up, you can promote it on social media or just wait for your earnings to come in as you prepare for the next course you create.

Some Tips to Remember

As you put your course material together, you will no doubt encounter difficulty. The key is to push forward, even if you do not feel very confident. As long as your course contains valuable information for your intended learners, you can be sure that it will get sold. Here are some other things you need to take note of:

1. **You do not need to be an expert.** The Internet is full of information that you can use in creating a course. You only need to organize this information in a smooth, flowing way that will give value to your target audience. So go ahead; pick the best information you can about your niche or subject and use it to your advantage.

2. **Your first few courses will not be perfect.** There might be something wrong with the video or audio, you may not sound very sure of what you are talking about, the editing will not be on point, and the result will not be as flawless as you expect, no matter how hard you have worked for it. It will not be the best online training course, but that is absolutely fine. You cannot expect yourself to get it right the first time. The important thing is to push yourself to become better in the subsequent courses you create. It goes without saying that you should evaluate your first courses for what went wrong and use your observations about how you can improve the next ones.

3. **Do your best to come up with the best course.** As much as possible, come up with the most professional looking courses. Use your own photos if you can, or use photos that are not copyrighted. If you will be using videos in the course, make sure that each video is only up to five minutes long, and can stand

alone as a tutorial on how to address a particular problem. Each video must be branded with your name, logo, photo or your website address. Make sure that you begin each video by outlining what you will do and that you end it by making a recap or telling your audience what you have just done.

4. **Technical skills are good to have, but are not a requirement.** You want to keep your costs to a minimum especially if you are just starting, so try to do all the work on your own. If you have a friend who can take care of the technical aspects of the course, then by all means have them shoot the videos you require or edit and polish the course. Otherwise, do not stress over your lack of technical skills. You yourself can learn the art of taking photos and videos and even editing the entire course. In the end, you will not have just produced a paid course; you will also have gained additional skills that you can someday make a course tutorial out of, as well.

5. **Appreciate and leverage the power of networking and collaboration.** Get to know other course producers and instructors. Not only will you be able to learn from each other; you will also be able to collaborate on some courses and promote each other's courses. You must also bank on the power of affiliates, who can do a good job of marketing your courses. The more promotions you get, the better your reach and your sales will be.

6. **Free courses are helpful.** Of course, you will want some compensation for your hard work, but if you want to have a huge following who buy your courses, you must make a name for yourself. To do this, you have to invest some of yourself by creating free courses for people to sample. If they consider your free courses valuable and helpful, they themselves will seek out your paid courses. Later on, when you already have a huge following, you can start charging new learners for this free course. You will not only be compensated for your work, but you will also have the recommendations and reviews of the learners who enjoyed it when it was still offered free of charge.

7. **Keep your learners engaged by interacting with them and giving them continuous support, updates and even free courses.** This will ensure that they give you good feedback and keep coming back for your courses.

Marketing the Idea

Even before launching your course, you must get the word out and build a buzz around it. You can do this through the following methods:

1. **Creating an email list.** If you do not have a website, build one. Make an offer your target cannot resist, like a free course or some valuable advice that will attract their interest. They could get a freebie in exchange for their email address, which will allow you to build a list of people you will be sending updates to. Through your emails or regular newsletters, you can provide snippets that will build up their excitement or give them insights about how valuable and helpful your paid course is going to be.

2. **Featuring teasers of your courses on YouTube.** Spark interest by teasing your target audience and highlighting the benefits they will get from availing of your course. To attract even more learners, you can include a discount link at the beginning of the video. It is also helpful to give discount coupons with an expiry date, in order to get your potential customers to act with urgency and purchase the course while the coupon is still valid.

3. **Using social media.** Create Facebook, Twitter, Instagram and LinkedIn accounts that will give you and your course the social presence you need. Bear in mind that these channels must not just be used for promoting your courses alone. Rather, you must use these social media networks to provide your target audience and existing followers content that they will find entertaining and useful. As such, your posts must be thought out well in order to provide value. These networks will also increase engagement through likes, comments and shares. So you must leverage content in all forms: texts, photos, audios and videos. The more people talk about you and your website, the higher your chances

of organically appearing in the SERPs. The more prominent your website is in the search results, the more widespread your niche and your products will be.

4. **Writing engaging content in articles and blogs.** We keep going on and on about content because it is what gives power to your site. The more engaging and attractive your posts and write-ups are, the higher your chances of ranking in the results pages of search engines. Of course, to do this, you must do proper keyword searches using the Google Keyword Planner Tool, as explained in IDEA 1.

CHAPTER 4:

IDEA 4 – Website Blogging

"Don't focus on having a great blog. Focus on producing a blog that's great for your readers."

-Brian Clark

If you have the least inclination whatsoever about writing, then you probably have tried blogging at one time or another. But life took place and you stopped posting to your blog. Looking back at that period of time, you are probably scratching your head and wondering why you did not continue blogging. Maybe you too could have been making money by now.

Still, you have this big question mark in your mind. Blogging as a business? Is that really possible? Many people think of blogs as a pastime, a side project or really just an online journal they can use to chronicle their daily lives, but the more enlightened ones have turned their blogs into a money-generating venture. You can read through Authorityhacker.com to see just how much the best bloggers are making and from where they get their revenue. Some personal bloggers have also sold their blogs to big corporations. Thus, blogging is not just a trend or a hobby. It is, in reality, a business model, and bloggers are not just hobbyists; they are entrepreneurs.

How Blogs Earn

How exactly does a blog earn? Generally, blogs earn from three areas: advertising, affiliate marketing and selling products and services. But before you earn from any of these, you must first establish a reputation, and your blog must be known as a provider of valuable content. Only through great content will you be able to generate the traffic that you need in order to monetize your blog. The higher traffic you have as a result of your effectively written content, the more prominent your blog will be in the search engines pages. The higher your ranking is, the more people are likely to visit your blog. The more visitors your blog gets, the greater your chances for earning.

Driving Traffic

Truth be told, great content is not all there is to get people flocking to your blog. You may be producing great content, but oftentimes this content gets drowned by the competition, of which there is a lot. Here are some tips you can use to drive traffic:

1. **Make your content visually appealing.** Well-written posts are great, but you need to break through the clutter of information available on the net and attract visitors. For this, you need visual content like videos, screenshots, photos, infographics, cartoons and even memes. All these visuals can aid reader engagement.

2. **Give your posts better titles.** Think catchy, striking and engaging titles. More often than not, readers will skip reading something with a boring title. So instead of giving your post the title "Five Christmas Cake Recipes," you can title it "Five Cake Recipes that will Make Your Christmas Merry."

3. **Share your content many times.** If you have shared it once, share it again. Many bloggers make the mistake of sharing their posts once on social media and then completely forgetting about it. Later on they wonder why the post did not get the exposure they expected. According to blog.kissmetrics.com it is perfectly fine to share a post more than once, using various social media channels. You probably think that sharing too much will seem like spamming, and it could, but the secret is in scheduling when you would share. Naturally, you will be sharing the content as soon as it is published on Twitter, Facebook, Google+, LinkedIn or any other social media account you have. You can share it again on Twitter two hours after, and then a day after. You can share the content again a week after you write the post, and then a month after. As for Facebook, you can share it again after a month. When you do re-share the content, make sure to use a different text, maybe a different hashtag. Re-sharing the content is important in reaching possible blog visitors who missed it the first time.

4. **Include links in your posts.** You can include links to previous posts of yours which are related to your current post, or a link to other blog posts and articles. Not only will these links work to help search engines index your content, it will also open the possibility of high quality websites linking back to you. When these high quality websites put a link of your blog on their page, you have better chances of ranking higher in the search results.

Including links will also help your readers get more information just by clicking on the links.

5. **Invite well-known people in your niche to write guest posts.** You want your blog to have a wider reach, so ask for help from well-known bloggers and prominent people within your niche. Not only will this produce good posts with great content for your readers; you will also draw the readers and followers of these bloggers. If they like what they see in your other posts, then you will get yourself new followers and readers. Plus, these bloggers can also link to some of your posts in the future when it is their turn to write in their own blogs or elsewhere. In a similar vein, you can also interview prominent people in your niche in order to get more readerships.

Making Money from Your Blog

If your blog has good enough traffic, then you can start monetizing it through the following:

1. **Advertising.** Blog advertisements work the same way as TV ads. When you have a lot of traffic on your blog, many products or services related to your blog's niche will vie for a place in your blog. To do this, you must sign up with an advertising network, the most popular of which is Google AdSense. Once you are approved for AdSense, you get a code which you can add to your website. This code allows Google to place ads on your page that are related to your blog posts. These ads can then appear as banners or images on your blog. When visitors to your blog click on these images or banners, you get paid a certain amount (less than a dollar to $2 per click) depending on the bids of those who put up their ads, the kind of content you have and other factors. You must not, however, expect to get rich quick with ads, unless you have very rich content and heavy traffic. Plus, if you are just starting out with not a lot of readers, it would help to put off signing up with Google AdSense and alternative advertising networks until you have established your blog.

Aside from displaying ad banners from advertising networks, you can also display private ads, or ads that you have directly negotiated with business owners themselves. You can choose to rent ad space on your blog to businesses that offer products and services related to your posts.

2. **Affiliate marketing.** We have already discussed affiliate marketing in detail as a way of earning money. This entails including links of products or services in your blog posts. When your readers click on these links and buy the products or services offered, you get a commission for the sale.

3. **Selling your own products and services.** If you have products of your own, then you can also advertise them in your blog. These products can be digital products like e-books, webinars, audio and video, photos or even membership to a club or group you have built. You can also offer physical products like craft items and handmade goods or services like event planning, babysitting or installations. You can also advertise virtual services that you offer like copywriting services, SEO, virtual assistance and the like.

Bear in mind that generating income from your blog is not easy; you need to invest your time and energy. You will not immediately earn from your blog, and you might even make mistakes. If that happens, you need to look at what went wrong and improve your next attempts.

Example Ideas

What must you write about? Most blogs start as a hobby, and this is all right. However, if you are thinking of starting a blog, why not see it as a way of generating an income stream separate from your day job or other business ventures? Of course, the choice of a niche or subject to blog about is important; it must be something that a lot of people want to read. Internet marketing and blogging is a hot topic nowadays, as more and more people are realizing that they can earn from it. If this kind of topic does not seem appealing to you, you can start a blog about something you are passionate about. The following are sample ideas you might be interested in:

- Parenting
- Playing a musical instrument
- Fiction and poetry writing
- DIY crafting
- Woodworking
- Traveling

Taking the Idea to Market

To start a blogging business, the first thing you need to do is to decide on the niche and your audience. Establishing this will guide you in the direction your blog is going to take. Here are the steps you should take in starting your blog:

1. **Decide on the domain name.** The domain name is your dot-com, dot-net, or dot-org name (also known as the web address). The best domain name is one that tells audiences what you are blogging about. If you are planning to have a blog on DIY crafting, you can choose diycrafternow.com as your domain name. You have to check for the availability of the domain name, as someone else may have chosen that name already.

2. **Choose a blogging platform and a web host.** WordPress is the most popular blogging platform there is. It offers both free hosting (wordpress.com) and self-hosting (wordpress.org).
   The web host houses all the files you have on your blog. You can choose to have free hosting, but your domain name will have the blogging platform name affixed. For example, if you opt for a WordPress.com account, your domain name would be diycrafter.wordpress.com. Free hosting is also not recommended, because this means your blog can be taken down anytime, as you do not really own it. If you opt for self-hosting, you can sign up (for a fee) with www.bluehost.com (highly recommended by WordPress) or its alternatives.

3. **Install your chosen blogging platform on the web host.** After signing up with the web host, you can now install Drupal, WordPress or whatever website of your choice, as long as the web host supports it.

4. **Customize your blog.** If you think blog design does not really matter, think again. As mentioned before, people are visual. A clean and crisply designed blog with great content will not just attract new visitors, it will also keep readers coming back for more. Make sure that its layout is optimized for readability, and that it is easy to navigate. Make sure to include buttons or widgets that will allow readers to share your content. Most blogging platforms like WordPress offer different themes; you can also customize the look of your blog or hire someone to do it.

5. **Write your first blog post.** It would be best to write an introductory post, one that would tell readers who you are, what your blog is about and what they can expect from the blog. Even if you are blogging for business, it does not hurt to show some personality. Again, one of the things you are after is the engagement of your would-be readers and followers. Of course, you must strike the balance between being too personal and being too formal. Make sure to edit and proofread your entry properly and encourage feedback from readers. You can ask them a question or ask for ideas about what they want to read on your subsequent posts. Do not rush your first post (or any other post) to make sure that you do not miss some points or say something you should not have.

6. **Schedule your blog posts.** There are no rules about how often you should post. Forbes states that you must post at least 16 times a month, while Writtent.com and Blogpress state that it depends on the kind of blog you are running. What all three agree on is that posting should be consistent. If you opt to post once a week on a Monday, make sure that you do so every Monday.

Marketing the Idea

Your blog will be generating its own traffic, so it is easy to be lazy and complacent that it will earn, just as long as you consistently post great content. However, the Internet is saturated with information: some helpful and valuable, some mostly just noise. So you must be aggressive in marketing your blog and getting the word out, especially if you are just starting. Here are some suggestions:

1. **Leverage your social media presence.** Social media, such as, Facebook especially, is a powerful tool you can use to reach your target audience, since most everyone uses social media every day. Twitter is also a great way of spreading the word, as well as LinkedIn. You can also make a short video which you can post on YouTube with a link that would direct people to your blog.

2. **Make a little investment in promoting your blog.** Is your audience always on Facebook? Then pay for Facebook ads once in a while so your ads will be targeted to users who are most likely to read your blog. You can also put up a campaign on Google AdWords to help boost your ranking in the SERP.

3. **Give freebies and hold contests.** Increase engagement through giveaways. You can ask readers and followers to comment on your blog or share your posts to social media. You then hold an electric raffle to choose a winner who will receive a prize from you or from sponsoring companies and businesses.

4. **Remind followers and readers about your upcoming post by sending regular newsletters.** Your newsletter does not have to promote anything, but it can include content your audience will find interesting and valuable. You do not even have to write the entire newsletter yourself; you can curate the best articles and write-ups from the Internet and share these with your followers. You can even ask questions or suggestions about what to include on your next blog posts. Your newsletter can also bring the attention of your readers to your earlier blog posts they might have missed.

5. **Be a guest blogger.** Look for other bloggers in your niche and reach out to them. Offer to write guest posts and invite them to write on your blog as well. This is a great way to make yourself known not just to other bloggers but to their respective followers and readers as well.

CHAPTER 5:

IDEA 5 – YouTube Business Channel

"You shouldn't focus on why you can't do something, which is what most people do. You should focus on why perhaps you can, and be one of the exceptions."

- Steve Case

Everyone who's someone is on YouTube. No wonder it is the most popular of all the video sites on the World Wide Web. It is so popular that the name has somehow become quite synonymous with Google. You want to watch a makeup tutorial? Go to YouTube. Do you want to see when Lisa Simpson spoke her first word? You YouTube it. Everyone knows what YouTube is; even a three year old can navigate her way through YouTube on her mother's smartphone.

It comes as no surprise that businesses both big and small are on YouTube too. With a billion active users per month, YouTube is a great vehicle for showcasing to the world the products and services a company have. YouTube is both a way of advertising products and services and an income generator in itself.

If you need another income stream, then producing YouTube videos just might be the thing for you. Not sure you have good enough content to gather views, likes and subscriptions? There are some kids who have used YouTube, though not even 12 years old, they already have hundreds of thousands to millions of subscribers. Of course, it helps that they are cute and adorable and that they have (enterprising) parents who film and edit their videos.

If kids can do it, so can you. Yes, you probably are not even the least bit cute now, but you have your wits and smarts about you. And if you use your creativity and resourcefulness, you too can earn from YouTube.

How to Earn Money from YouTube

If you are a new YouTuber, the first thing you need to do is to establish yourself as a video creator. You cannot just create an account and expect the money to roll in. Just like the home-based business ideas presented earlier, earning from YouTube will come later on after you have built a following from creating content-rich videos that people want to watch. According to The Young Turks COO Steven Oh, as more than just a video site, YouTube is a tool for social engagement. When you produce quality content, you will attract viewers and subscribers. When your reach and viewership gets wide enough, then you can start earning from your YouTube channel through the following methods:

1. **Advertisements with Google AdSense (becoming a YouTube partner)**. One thing you must understand about YouTube is that it is not a get-rich-quick scheme. As CTNtechnology explains, you will not get paid every time someone watches your videos; you only get paid when the person watching your video watches or clicks on the ad that comes with your videos. Neither will you get paid if someone subscribes to your channel or comments on or likes your videos. However, these subscriptions, likes and comments are helpful for creators because these activities tell Google that the You Tuber is actually producing great content. When you have a monetized channel with great content, then Google will be sending ads to your channel, which can help you earn.

   To understand how much a YouTuber can possibly make, you need to familiarize yourself with the following:

   - **CPM (cost per mille).** This refers to the amount a video creator earns per 1000 ad views. Note that it is the number of "ad" views, not video views. The rate (usually ranging from less than $1 to $5) depends on how many advertisers are willing to put their ads on the videos, and how much these advertisers pay.
   - **CPC (cost per click).** This refers to the rate an advertiser pays when a viewer clicks on their ad shown on your video.
   - **CPV (cost per view).** This refers to the rate an advertiser will pay when their ad appears on your video. This rate is lower than CPC.
     All these rates vary not just according to the advertisers' budget, but also on how great your content is, or under what category or niche your videos fall (for example, advertisers in the health niche pay higher than those in the fashion niche).
   - **Advertising formats.** The ads that run with your videos come in different formats. Advertisers pay varying rates for these ads.

- HowCast. This channel boasts of 7 channels that feature different categories like gaming, food and healthy living, among others. The main channel alone has 4.9 million subscribers and more than 2.5 billion views.

1. **Comedy videos.** Everyone loves a good laugh, and YouTube provides a lot of laughs, thanks to its many users that showcase skits and comedy videos. If you know how to tickle the funny bone, then maybe you can join the ranks of these popular video creators:

   - HowToBasic. Despite the channel name, HowToBasic is not a tutorial channel in the conventional sense. While not a lot of people might find the videos in this channel agreeable, it has certainly gained the attention of a lot of YouTube viewers, which explains its 8,436,679 subscribers and 1.2 billion views.
   - llSuperwomanll. Lilly Singh is a Canadian YouTuber known for her funny skits. With 10.6 million subscribers and 1.6 billion views, it is no wonder that she is considered one of the most popular YouTube personalities.

2. **Product reviews.** Technology has made many things possible, including the ease by which products and services can be delivered. Nowadays, people have so many choices it has become rather difficult to decide which product to buy or which service to use. This is why product reviews are very popular.

   - **Tested.** 2,269,473. This is how many subscribers this channel has. Launched in 2010 by Will Smith and Norman Chan and joined in by Adam Savage of Mythbusters. This channel makes reviews on just about anything these creators find awesome, which works for them, as the site has 411,143,622 views already, and counting.
   - **CNET.** This technology YouTube site features reviews for all things tech – computers, laptops, smartphones, you name it. The channel currently has 1,285,894 subscribers and 6.8 million views.

3. **Vlogs.** You surely are not Patrick Starfish, so you know what a vlog (or a video log) is. Vlogs are where people talk about anything and everything in their daily lives. People are generally nosy, which probably explains the attraction to vloggers. If you are naturally a talkative or funny, you might want to try vlogging. Of course, it is a must that the things you talk about are entertaining and engaging.

   - **SHAYTARDS.** This channel features the daily lives of a family, Shay Carl and Colette Butler and their kids. Not only are their videos funny and entertaining; they are also radiating with positivity and love. No wonder they have 4.8 million subscribers and 2.5 billion views.

   - **JoeyGraceffa.** This channel has 7.2 million subscribers, 1.1 billion views. Joey Graceffa updates his channel almost every day, with his fun, funny and entertaining takes on microwaving Sharpies, drawing his life and googling himself, among others. He also has short films in his channel, music videos, and promotional videos for other things he does, like writing books.

4. **Gaming.** Although gaming was only a little known niche once upon a time on YouTube, it has grown exponentially over the past years. If you are a gamer and like getting your hands on the newest games and testing them out, you can create a YouTube channel and tell people about these games, like the following top gaming You Tubers do:

   - **Pewdiepie.** This is not just the most subscribed gaming channel on YouTube. It is the most subscribed YouTube channel, ever with 51.7 million subscribers and 14 billion views. No one knows exactly what channel creator Flix Kjllberg's formula for success is, but it sure is working.

   - **VanossGaming.** YouTube creator Evan Fong churns out humorous and entertaining gaming videos (mostly horror games) with high production quality. If you do not believe this, then just ask his 19.5 million subscribers who have given his channel 6.4 billon views.

Taking the Idea to Market

Ready to try your hand at entertaining and engaging people through YouTube and earning revenue from doing so? Follow these steps:

Creating Your YouTube Channel

1. **Create your free Google account** (if you do not have one yet). Unless you have a Google account, you will not be able to sign in to YouTube.

2. **Sign in to YouTube using your Google account.** Go to youtube. com and sign in with your Google account username and password.

3. **Go to your YouTube account settings.** Click on your account profile picture on the top right corner of your screen (this will appear as a generic person icon if you have not added your display photo yet). Click on the Creator Studio button.

4. **Create your YouTube channel.** On the Creator Studio page, you will see a list of drop down menus on the left side panel. Click on Channel. You will see Status and Features on the upper part of the centre of the page. Click on the Verify button under your Google account email.

   You will be brought to a page that says "Use YouTube as..." where you can change the name or leave it as you prefer.

   The page also has a link for creating a brand account or a business name.

   Click Create Channel.

5. **Customize your YouTube page.** Add your channel art to the top of the page and put in your channel description. If you have a website, it would be best to make the channel art similar to that of your website to stimulate recall in viewers. You can also customize the privacy and layout of your channel by clicking on the Settings icon on the right side of the page, below the Channel Art panel.

Uploading Videos

Remember that at this stage, your main aim is to gain subscribers, viewers, likes and comments. So you must produce videos that are highly entertaining and engaging. Here are some tips:

- **Think your video concepts through.** Plan and design the direction they are going to take by knowing what you are shooting before you shoot, especially if you are just starting. Even vloggers should have an idea of what they are to going to talk about and what they will say even before they start filming. If you do not do this, you might end up spending lot of time editing your videos.
- **Use an HD camera.** While camera smartphones are getting better and better with every new release, it still pays to have a high definition camera that you can use to record your video.
- **Get good lighting.** Your content may be good and you may have one of the best hi-res cameras, but if your lighting is so-so, your videos will not come out looking their best.
- **Invest in high quality audio.** No one wants to watch videos with poor, squeaky or scratchy audio. While a generic microphone works okay, you want your viewers to enjoy watching your videos that are not just pleasing to the eyes but to the ears as well.
- **Edit your videos.** You can use Windows Movie Maker or iMovie, which come free with Windows computers and Macs, but you can also use paid editing software.

Scheduling Posts

You have the ability to set the videos as public, unlisted or private. Of course, you want to have as many viewers as possible, so set your videos to public. However, if you are not sure that it is time to post the video for public viewing, then you might want to set it to private first. This feature also allows you to upload all the video content you want without worry.

Unlisted videos cannot be seen by anyone, unless they have the link to those videos.

If you are already a YouTube Partner, you can also schedule your videos to be published at pre-specified times as part of your strategy and marketing. After uploading your video, you can customize its settings by going to the Basic Info window and setting the date, time and time zone and clicking the Publish button. The video will be published at the scheduled time.

Monetizing Your Videos

Here are the steps to follow so you can start earning from your videos. You must, however, be aware of the requirements for monetizing videos.

1. **Be a YouTube partner.** To do this, you must log in to your YouTube account, click the "Creator Studio" button and click "Status and Features" under the drop down item "Channel" on the panel on the left of the page. Click "Enable" under "Monetization" and read and accept the terms and conditions of the YouTube Partner Program.

2. **Set up an AdSense account.** Follow the prompts to set up your AdSense account by signing in with your Google account information. Wait for the approval of your AdSense account, which take around 48 hours.

3. **Choose the videos you want to monetize.** You can do this to monetize both the old and new videos in your channel. You also have the ability to monetize multiple videos at once.

Marketing the Idea

Ideally, YouTube generates its own traffic. However, you can make your channel even more popular by sharing your video content to various channels like Facebook, Twitter, Instagram and LinkedIn, among others. The more views, shares, likes and comments you get, the greater your reach spreads.

You can also post text or visual content in your website or blog that contains links to our videos. Of course, it is important that the content is related to the videos. Otherwise, you will lose your credibility and be seen as a spammer.

CHAPTER 6:

IDEA 6 – Being an Outsourcer

"If you deprive yourself of outsourcing and your competitors do not, you're putting yourself out of business."

-Lee Kuan Yew

The Skinny on Outsourcing

Businesses are ever evolving, thanks to the continuous developments in technology. In the past, starting and running a business involved a lot of investment, especially time and money. Nowadays, anyone who has an idea for a product or service, a little capital, and a lot of smarts can successfully start and run a business.

One of the strategies that arose in answer to the challenges of today's businesses is outsourcing, or the process of hiring another company or individual to do the job. This practice allows business processes that are usually done in-house to be accomplished by a freelancer, or someone who is not a part of the company for a fee. Both big and small companies have been using outsourcing as an effective way of doing business for the following reasons:

Cheaper Labour, same quality of work. Startup companies that do not have the finances of big businesses must turn to outsourcing to get work done. For example, a small company can outsource a freelancer to do internet marketing for them. The startup only needs to post the opening on websites like Upwork

- **Zero employee benefits.** A freelancer gets paid only for the work he does, upon his agreement with the business owner or employer. And because he is not really a part of the company, he does not need to be paid extra for medical benefits or insurance. The freelancer would also have to use his own resources, such as, laptop, internet connection, software or apps needed for the job. This results in big savings for companies that outsource, since they do not need to provide these needs.
- **Non-payment for idle time.** In an office, you cannot expect all employees to be bent down on their desks day in and day out. They have coffee breaks that come with the unavoidable chitchat, meetings that go on for up to an hour (or more), time spent looking through emails and answering them. All through these activities, the company pays its workers regardless of their productivity. When they outsource, businesses are able to avoid big overhead

costs not just on the salary, but also on the electric bill, internet bill, building rent and other miscellaneous expenses.

- **Expertise.** Many freelancers have a lot of experience in their field of specialization. It is not surprising for a business to find a freelancer who has previously worked on the same project for another client or company. As such, the freelancer knows exactly what he is doing and does it really well so the business can really get its money's worth.

It is not only companies that outsource work. Even individual entrepreneurs sometimes make use of outsourcing, not just to save on costs but also to save time. They outsource the tasks they are not good at to people who can so they do not have to spend a considerable amount of time learning how to do the task. Instead, they can use their time wisely on other aspects of their business.

Why Be an Outsourcer?

With businesses mushrooming left and right, it is no surprise that being an outsourcer has become a lucrative business. It is so profitable that some people who started freelancing as a side job have come to leave their 9-5 jobs for the comfort of working on their own laptops wherever they may be, for example, in an internet café, in the neighborhood coffee shop, or in their makeshift home office, without having to get dressed or do their hair and makeup.

The setup proves very appealing for parents as well – they can earn without having to leave their children in someone else's care. And just like any other home-based business, being an outsourcer allows you to save on childcare costs, gas money and other miscellaneous expenses.

Being an Outsourcer: Do You Have What it Takes?

If there is one thing you have to know before plunging headlong into becoming an outsourcer or freelancer, it is the fact that freelancing is not for everyone. You might be attracted to having no boss to answer to, or the amount that you can save from not having to commute or to drive to work every day, but you must possess certain characteristics if you are to survive being in this business.

You must also know that being an outsourcer does not save you from the stresses you normally associate with a corporate job. For one, you would still be working; you would be dealing with their clients, their demands and their requirements. The only difference is that you would not have a boss as a middleman between you and the client and no officemates to distract you or provide help when you need it.

The pay as an outsourcer will not necessarily be better than your corporate job salary, since you will only be paid for the work you do. If your work is not satisfactory, you will have to fix it, but you will not be compensated for the time you spent righting your mistakes, unlike in your 9-5 job, where you receive the same salary regardless if you screw-up on a task. You also would have to go through the process of paying taxes yourself, which is something a corporate employer does for its employees through salary deductions.

That said, here are some of the things required of you, should you plan to be an outsourcer:

1. **Experience, experience, experience.** If you are entering the home-based picture as an outsourcer of a service that you used to provide previously, then all well and good. But if you are arriving in the scene as a greenhorn, then you most likely will struggle to succeed. Of course, you need to prove to prospective clients why they should hire your services. If you have nothing to show, then try something else, or build your portfolio first to proof that you have the skills they need.

2. **Self-discipline.** Being an outsourcer requires big amounts of discipline and time management skills. If you are juggling household chores, taking care of your kids and working online, you must set a schedule when you can work undisturbed. And even then, you must discipline yourself and make sure you stick to the task at hand and not let yourself get distracted by social media sites or games on your computer.

   On the other side of the spectrum, you must also take care not to overwork yourself, which can cause burn out in the long run.

When you work at home, you will not have a set time for taking breaks or going home, so if you are the workaholic type, you must learn to pace yourself.

3. **Motivation.** Self-discipline is not enough; you must also find motivation that will drive you to fulfil your tasks the best way you can. The danger of working from home is that you can become lazy and complacent, which will in turn cause you to be mediocre at what you do. If you cannot give the best without a boss to manage or motivate you, then you have to think twice, even thrice, about giving up your corporate job for an outsourcer stint.

4. **A network of people who know what you do.** This is important in building your reputation as an outsourcer. The more people who know your skills and how you deliver, the better your chances of getting more clients. You must also have the knack for finding clients; otherwise, you will not have any luck working as a freelancer. Unless you have a steady stream of clients, you will not have a steady income. e

5. **People skills.** Working from home does not mean you won't have to deal with people. While there is no pressure to be friends with the people at work, you still have to talk to a lot of clients, especially if you happen to be in the customer service field.

6. **A professional image.** When you work for a company, it is the company's brand that you represent. As an outsourcer, you are your own brand, so it is important that you remain professional all the time, especially in your social media presence. As you bid for jobs, potential clients could be looking you up on the internet, so it would be wise to keep your private life offline.

7. **A quiet place to work.** Sure you can work in the kitchen or in your bedroom. However, it is best to have a space that is dedicated just for work. You do not even need an entire room or office (although this would be ideal); you can just set up a workstation in some quiet place free of distraction. This way, you get to separate work from your daily life. If you have kids, you could establish boundaries. So that when they see Mummy or Daddy sitting in their "office," they have to keep quiet and play elsewhere.

If you have these requirements, then being an outsourcer might just be the right career for you. To start, you must first decide on the kind of service you want to offer.

Example Ideas

Outsourcers provide different kinds of services, from designing and creating websites to writing press releases. And then there are different odd jobs that would require you to do physical work like walking dogs, cleaning houses, babysitting, woodworking, picking up stuff and other occupations you can find on websites such

Generally, outsourcers provide the following services, among others:

- **Data entry and transcription jobs.** Many clients need audio transcribed into text. These jobs are probably the easiest you can start with, especially if you are just intending to be an outsourcer on the side.
- **Translation jobs.** If you are good at languages, you can find jobs that need you to translate text from English to another language or vice versa.
- **Online tutoring.** Many Korean, Japanese and Chinese learners want to study and enhance their English language skills, making this job quite profitable. There are also clients who need help with their academic subjects and/or other fields of study.
- **Internet marketing and SEO.** This is perhaps one of the most in-demand jobs. But there are also a lot of competitors, so if this is what you want to do, you must deliver exceptional quality to break through the competition.
- **Admin support, back office and virtual assistance.** Many small businesses do not have the capability to do admin tasks due to budget constraints, so there are a lot of clients seeking these services.
- **Customer Service, inbound, telemarketing and sales and outbound cold calling.** Similarly, some companies do not have in-house customer or sales representatives. Even big corporations outsource their customer service, so why shouldn't small companies follow suit?

- **Web design, development and creation.** Many businesses are being created by the day, and business owners know how important it is to have a website and an internet presence. This is why web designers and creators are very popular.
- **Accounting and human resources management.** These functions need not be done in-house, so business owners have taken to outsourcing people to do these tasks as well.
- **Digital product creation.** If you are good at developing information-based products such as e-books, podcasts or audiobooks, you can be an outsourcer and make these materials for clients if you do not want to sell them on your own.

Getting Started

Convinced that being an outsourcer is perfect for you? Then let the following guide you in starting your outsourcing business:

1. **Decide on your niche.** When choosing the kind of service you want to offer, you must, of course, take into consideration the skills that you have. If you are well versed in the financial field, then you can work as a consultant for people who want to achieve financial freedom. If your forte is administrative tasks, then you can market yourself as a virtual assistant. You can teach online English if you have grammar and structure skills that foreign learners need. The idea is to maximize the skills that you have.

   You must also decide on the scope of service you are offering. If you want to be a freelance writer, would you be offering copywriting or editing services as well? Would you include writing white papers, infographics and e-books, or would you focus on writing SEO articles?

2. **Study the market.** Which skills are in demand right now? Which of these in-demand skills do you have? How will you be able to use your existing skills as an outsourcer? You can do this through online search, by using Google AdWords, in the same way you would conduct a search of the market demand in the other ideas presented in this book.

Similarly, you can do a survey in your locality. Which small businesses need outsourcing and what kind of services do they need? Based on these needs, you can make a pitch about how you can solve some of their problems through outsourcing. Of course, you must be ready with answers to questions business owners may have, including price quotes.

3. **Write a business plan.** It does not matter if you will be handling the business alone, doing it with a partner or with a group of people. There are many business plan templates you can find on the internet, but when it comes down to it, your plan must contain the essentials of the business you want to put up: your business goals, the financial requirements of your business and how you could market your plan and bring it into action.

   You might argue that you can be an outsourcer without all these details since there is nothing to plan. However, if you wish to make it big as an outsourcer, you need to plan your strategies, especially if you are not able to achieve your initial goals. You must also be ready to pivot or to abandon your goals for another line of business if it does not work out.

4. **Build your network.** Use the internet to make yourself known in your niche. Join forums, ask questions and answer questions if you can. This will not just help you learn more about what you will be doing; it will also make you known in the circle of experts, outsourcers and even business owners. The more you get known, the larger your network grows. Start a blog and use it to share what you are learning and encourage interaction by asking questions.

5. **Learn the ropes.** It would be very helpful to learn as much as you can about the business you are starting. While the internet is a rich source of information, nothing beats getting your information and know-how from a professional in the field. In order to do this, you must keep growing your network and proving that you have what it takes to be successful. At some point, an expert will take notice of you and help you launch your business by referring you to clients.

6. **Sign up on freelancing websites.** Join freelance websites like Upwork.com, which will give you access to thousands of outsourcing jobs that you can do. While the competition may be tough, you will surely find a client with whom you can agree and deal with.

7. **Grow your business.** Some outsourcers do not just stay as outsourcers; they go on to build their own businesses, which can take in other outsourcers. This is why you need a business plan, so you will have a vision and a goal-which, hopefully, is to establish your brand and the services you offer.

Marketing the Idea

In order to profit from this home-based business idea, you must know how to market yourself. Here are some suggestions about how you can spread the word about your business and the services you offer:

1. **Create a marketing plan.** Just as it is in establishing your business, you must also have a marketing plan. This plan must include your target clients, how strong the competition is, what you can do to differentiate the services you offer from that of the competition, and what strategies you will use to reach your target market.

2. **Establish your personal brand.** As mentioned previously, as an outsourcer, you represent nothing and no one but yourself. This is why you must develop a good reputation as a great provider of outsourced services. Leverage the power of social media sites such as LinkedIn, Facebook, Twitter, Google+, Quora and other similar sites. You must also attend conferences, seminars and talks personally, so you can expose yourself to others. Of course, if you are just starting and need to make a name for yourself, you might be called to do big tasks for small amounts of income, so you must be ready for this too. This way, you can build your portfolio while making yourself known in the community.

3. **Contact everyone you know and let them know of your new business.** It takes some time to be able to get new clients and

to have steady and regular clients who give you repeat business. So even before you fully launch yourself into selling your services, make sure you have advertised yourself to anyone and everyone you know. While your best friend, your neighbour or the friendly grocer down the street might have no need for a web designer, they might know someone who does. And if you have been diligently doing number two above, you will eventually find clients who have probably heard of you and are willing to try your services.

4. **Be your best.** There is no better way of marketing your services than by word-of-mouth and referrals from old clients. If you consistently perform and do the tasks given to you efficiently, clients will be happy with your work. This increases the likelihood of them hiring you again for future projects and referring you to other potential clients. You will also get more positive reviews, which will up your client base. The more you get known in the field, the better your reputation. You can then start charging higher rates or forming a bigger group (such as an outsourcing agency) to take on more work as a result of your initial hard work.

5. **Use common and usual marketing strategies.** These include the strategies mentioned in the first few business ideas already presented above: write a blog with regularly updated content powered by in-demand words and phrases as those from your search results in Google AdWords, offer to write guest posts for similarly-themed blogs and websites, use Facebook, Instagram, Twitter and other social media sites to spread your content and your brand. When your business has got bigger and you start earning more, you can also advertise through Google AdWords, Facebook ads or through affiliate marketing.

CHAPTER 7:

IDEA 7 – Being a Freelance Writer

"When everything seems to be going against you, remember that the airplane takes off against the wind, not with it."

-Henry Ford

Making money as a freelance writer seems easy enough; all you need is a computer with internet access and a knack for writing. If it is your lack of experience, or the fear that you are not good enough, that is keeping you from trying writing as an income source, then you must know that you need only your horse sense (and your writing craft, of course) to be able to succeed as a freelance writer.

The internet offers infinite work opportunities for freelance writers. Because of the availability of writing jobs, talented writers who are committed and disciplined will find freelance writing gigs very lucrative.

Why should you be a freelance writer?

If you are not sure whether or not this is the home-based opportunity you are waiting for, here are five of the many reasons people do freelance writing:

1. **The demand for writing jobs is endless.** Websites need content articles that will drive visitors to their page, businesses require web copy, news sites will always be in need of news reports, and the list goes on. A freelance writer who knows where to find the best assignments will never be out of a job – or income.

2. **Freelance writing gives you greater flexibility.** If you are just starting to consider working from home, freelance writing can slowly ease you into the transition. You can still keep your day job as you start freelance writing on the side in your own time. Even if you get many clients and eventually quit your 9-5, you can still schedule writing to make room for other things like family outings or other work from home ventures.

3. **You do not need writing experience.** While there are some clients that will ask to see some of your published work, many will give you an assignment after seeing some of your writing samples – even if they have never been published. Being a freelance writer does not require a college degree either; as long as you know how to do your research and string ideas together using correct grammar and proper sentence construction, you will do great as a writer.

4. **Being a freelance writer can and will help you learn a lot of things.** As you take in different jobs from various clients, you will have to read up a lot, especially if you are asked to produce content regarding things, concepts and ideas you know nothing about. While this can seem tasking and exhausting at times, it certainly helps to have a lot of know-how. Being knowledgeable about a lot of things will not just help you in future writing assignments; it will also boost your confidence and make you feel good about yourself.

5. **The pay is good.** Do not get us wrong here. As a beginner, you will probably start writing for content mills that pay you a measly $5 per 500-word article, and this is all right. But as you gain experience, confidence and a network of clients satisfied with your work, you can start charging more. Of course, some clients will not want to pay a higher price when they could pay someone else a lower amount, but this is how you weed out jobs you do not want to do. By producing great output, you can get better paying clients for a high quality of work.

Why shouldn't you be a freelance writer?

There are a lot of advantages to being a freelance writer, sure, but there are also drawbacks – things that will make you want to think twice, such as:

1. **You have to look for work all the time.** As a freelance writer, you will get paid per contract or per piece. Even though there is a great demand for writers like you, these writing assignments will not just fall into your lap. Unless you find a client who wants you to work for them long-term, you always have to be on your toes finding clients to write for. You can take a break from finding clients to write for, yes, but this would also mean taking a break from making money.

2. **There is a lot of competition.** Because it is easy to be a freelance writer, you will find a lot of competition that will offer their services at lower prices. Of course, clients do want to take advantage of

these low prices. If you are a really talented writer, your work will speak for itself and you will be able to rise up from the content mill. You can bag higher paying gigs and assignments, never having to worry about competition anymore.

3. **You must work long hours.** If there is one thing freelance writers have to work against, it is the deadlines set by their clients. Sure, a writer can choose a time to do his work and prioritize everything else, but at the end of the day he still has to meet his deadlines. So he goes on a writing spree and works extended hours in order to turn his work in on time.

4. **There are no benefits.** If you have left your 9-5 for a home-based gig, then you will definitely lose all the benefits you used to enjoy from the company you were with. You have to pay for your own healthcare and insurance, plus you have to take care of your taxes, something your company used to do for you. There is no paid leave, either. If you want a vacation, then you can take a vacation anytime you want. However, you cannot expect to get any income while you are on break.

5. **You need to advertise and market yourself.** As a freelance writer, you are on your own. It is up to you how to get clients that will pay you at the rates you prefer. If you do not get clients, you will not be able to write and you will not have any income, unlike when you work on your day job, where you sit at a desk, wait for the boss to tell you what to do and get a steady monthly income regardless of the volume of work given to you.

If you are new to freelance writing, you might feel overwhelmed at the amount of work you need to put in – especially at the beginning. But then, that is how most people feel when they have a new job, or are just starting with a new company. As a new freelance writer, you need to find your footing through trial and error, especially when it comes to the kind of writing that you will do and the rates that you will charge. It would be best to do your research, and to join forums and frequent blogs that other freelance writers visit so you can get a feel of the business. You can also network with other writers and ask for insights to help you get started.

Example Ideas

Freelance writing takes many forms. You can be a jack-of-all trades, or you can focus on one area and be an expert on it. That said, here are some of the different writing jobs freelance writers can earn from:

1. **Web content.** Content is king, or so everyone who is marketing and advertising on the internet says. It is true, though. In order to attract customers, a website must have great content. This could be in the form of blogs, news reports, video clips or press releases. The main aim of content writers is to attract attention and engage customers in order to bring traffic to a website. The ultimate aim, of course, is to turn these website visitors into paying customers.

2. **Web copy.** While almost synonymous with web content, web copy is more focused on persuading readers to take action; that is, to buy a product or a service. Web copy could refer to blog posts (that lead to sales), updates on social media, product descriptions and advanced content like e-books, white papers and user guides.

3. **Blog posts.** Writing for blogs is probably one of the easiest ways to get into online writing. Many businesses and companies are looking for bloggers who will provide a steady stream of posts in order to attract and engage customers. Although not very lucrative (blogging jobs do not pay much), blogging can be your stepping stone to higher-paying gigs, especially if you have your name up there on the by-line.

4. **News writing.** No, you do not actually need to go out in the field and get the latest scoop, but you probably need to be glued to your computer and get information about the latest news as it comes, put a different spin on it and submit it for publishing.

5. **Feature writing.** If you are working for an online magazine, then you can go into feature writing. This can include human interest stories, info articles, personality sketches, or even personal experiences. Of course, the kind of writing you will produce must be consistent with the magazine's theme or topic.

6. **Product description writing.** Businesses with products to offer need someone to write descriptions for these products, such as those found in product catalogues. This can also take the form of product reviews and product comparisons.

7. **Technical Writing.** If you do well understanding how computers, smart phones and their peripherals work and can translate these seemingly intelligible terms into something the average Joe could easily digest, then you would do a good job of being a technical writer. Of course, as a technical writer, you would be also called upon to write about topics for techies.

There are other kinds of writing work that you will be asked to do. It is up to you to decide whether you want to be a generalist and write about anything and everything under the sun, or focus on a niche and gain experience and expertise in one area.

Taking the Idea to Market

Ready to plunge into the world of freelance writing? Here are some suggestions to get you started:

1. **Look for freelance writing jobs advertised on sites like upwork. com, or by signing up for content mills and other job boards**. The Writer Life lists job boards that can help you land jobs. While Craigslist does not seem an ideal place to score assignments, some writers have actually landed great gigs through craigslist. com. You just need to be patient and wade through the different posts and offers for writers. As for Upwork, you must sign up as a member before you can browse the different jobs on the site. There are also many websites that pay writers for their contributions, such as those listed in the blog in Make a Living Writing by Jennifer Roland.

2. **Start pitching.** When you find a writing job that you are comfortable doing, you can start responding to the ad, offering the prospective client details about how you will go about the assignment and your rates. When you write your proposal, make sure to include information about how you found out about the job

post, who you are and how you can help the prospective client get the desired results. Sometimes, the client specifies the rate and the deadline, as well as other details of the assignment. One of the best ways to get the client to hire you is by writing a sample that is highly related to the assignment. This will help put you on top of your competitors, especially if you are bidding for the job.

Once you have landed a few writing gigs, you will be able to feel your way around. When you have developed the confidence that you need and improved on your writing craft, you can be more aggressive and turn freelancing into a full-time business.

3. **Create a business plan.** Write down your goals for the business, and how you are going to reach these goals through a five-year plan. Your business plan must include the kind of niche you want to focus on, how you will get clients, how much your projected income is, and how you will build a reputation that will help you become an expert that businesses will turn to when they need something written. As you run your writing business, you will find that you sometimes have to deviate from your plan. Still, it will be a great help to have a framework to guide you as you work toward your business goals.

4. **Market yourself.** Many freelance writers are able to pay their bills just through their writing gigs. But this does not mean that anyone and everyone who is a freelance writer will end up in the same situation. No matter how good a writer you are and how professional you are when it comes to meeting deadlines and delivering quality work, you will not hit six figures a year (yes, this is possible) if you are not going to put yourself out there.

Marketing the Idea

How exactly do you market yourself? Of course, there is always Google AdWords. You can pay Google so your website can appear in a prominent place in the SERPs, but why would you want to pay for advertising when you can do it free through the following?

1. **Signing up in Upwork, Guru, and other similar sites.** Many businesses turn to these sites for help when they need to outsource work. As long as you have an active profile on these sites, any interested client can reach out to you and offer you a writing job. Also, through these sites, you can view different open jobs that you can bid on. However, you have a lot of competition here, especially if there are many bids on the same project you are pitching on. Still, this is a great way to start getting jobs and honing yourself as a writer.

2. **Blogging.** In order to build a reputation, you need to have an online presence. What could be better than having your own website with a blog section that can showcase your writing? By writing great content, you can drive not just a lot of traffic (which can also give you revenue through ads that would buy space in your blog), but also potential clients.

   Offer to write guest posts, and ask other freelancers to post on your blog – this will be a win-win for both parties, as readers (potential clients included) of the other blog can find you and check out your work and vice versa.

   You must also develop a by-line by writing on high traffic-sites, making sure that your writing bears your name. There are many great writers who do ghost writing. The pay is okay, but these writers remain anonymous and therefore do not get the opportunity as those who have made a name as freelancers.

3. **Social media.** Writing great content on your blog is not enough. You also need to spread the word through different channels, including social media. You could join Facebook groups, answer questions in different forums like Quora and even tweet about the services you offer. You could also make use of LinkedIn, which is a rich source of great writing gigs.

4. **Networking.** Aside from joining forums, you can also build friendships with other freelance writers. Not only will you be able to share best practices with them, they could also refer clients to you.

You can also build relationships offline. If there are events or conferences coming up in your area that pertain to your niche, you should sign up and go. You will not just gain more knowledge and skill about your area of focus, you also get the opportunity to meet and network with potential clients.

Additional Tips

Being a writer can seem pretty straightforward; after all, you only need a thirst for knowledge, an eye for what clicks and a way of putting words together. However, banking on your writing skills alone is not enough. You must also develop a business acumen that can help you land many writing gigs. Here are some more suggestions you can follow:

- **Decide on a niche.** There is nothing wrong with being a freelance writer who can write about a lot of topics. However, you can build a more solid client base if you focus on an area or two to specialize in. The more you build yourself as an expert, the bigger your chances of finding businesses that need your writing expertise. It also helps if you build your niche around something you are passionate about. Whether it is computers, parenthood or money matters, you will more easily find clients and an audience that will require your specialty.
- **Understand your client and your audience.** What kind of results does your client want? How will you be able to reach your audience? You must find a common ground between these two things and then focus your writing there. This way, you will be able to establish a connection with your audience, which will lead to their engagement.
- **Learn the art of negotiation.** You might agree to get $5 for every 300-word article, but as soon as you gain a proper footing, you must be able to adjust your rates. If you keep on staying on the rates you started with, you will never be able to live on writing alone, and you are missing on more money you might be making. If the potential client haggles or disagrees, do not push. You are better off writing for another client who will pay you for the quality of writing you produce.

- **Avoid scams like the plague.** There are many "clients" looking for writers to deliver articles for them, but do not fulfil their end of the bargain – they either pay half (which is the usual practice, as most writers ask for a 50% deposit before they start working), or do not pay at all. These clients ask for a sample article, saying they need to gauge the writer's tone or style, and after the article has been delivered, the writer never hears from them again. You must protect yourself; after all, this is a business. Be ready with your portfolio so you do not have to give free writing samples. Prepare a contract that states all your terms, including payment, delivery schedule, copyright on the work, and other similar items. Have the client sign the contract to make sure that he agrees with the terms.

- **Read, read and read.** As a writer, you have to continually build your knowledge, especially in your niche. Make it a habit to visit sites about your niche and read about your focus area and topics related to it. This way, you do not just increase your knowledge; you will also be able to provide your followers more value through the information you continuously gain.

CHAPTER 8:

IDEA 8 – Being a Website Consultant

"If somebody offers you an amazing opportunity but you are not sure you can do it,

Say yes – then learn how to do it later!"

- Richard Branson

What is a website consultant? Most people think that website consulting is about designing a website, but it is more than that. Website consulting involves a plethora of skills that allows web consultants to deal with anything and everything related to making a website function optimally, which includes development, design, strategy, marketing and even SEO. The long and short of it is that a website consultant is a jack-of-all-trades when it comes to maximizing the use of a website.

Tasks Website Consultants Do.

Most web consultants start as web design experts, branching later on to include marketing and SEO in their list of specializations. What does it take to be a web consultant? Here are some of the responsibilities a website consultant carries on his shoulders, tasks you would need to take on if you do decide to become one:

1. **Give website owners advice.** Advice on what? A lot of things. Is the website working optimally? Does it deliver a smooth user experience? How does the bigger picture look? Will it be able to bring in a lot of traffic and conversions? If not, then what should be done about it? More often than not, a business owner is too attached to his website; he only sees how good the site looks and does not realize that the reason his business is not picking up might be the website. Being hired as a web consultant means giving your clients advice on what should be done to their websites in order to maximize their performance, which will bring in revenue for the site owners.

2. **Identify and fix errors on the website.** What kind of errors could there possibly be? All kinds, from the simplest spelling errors you could fix in a day by simply going through the entire website content (which can be a lot, mind you), to duplicate content, to slow-loading pages. As a web consultant, it is your job to point these errors out and have them corrected.

3. **Evaluate the website.** If the website is not performing the way it is supposed to, should it be rebuilt? Or would some tweaking here and there do the job? Part of your tasks as a website consultant

is to size up the website and to explain to your client what needs to be done.

4. **Listen to the clients vent.** Your work as a consultant will not be limited to the website itself. A big part of your job will be focused on talking to your client, asking for his goals and his challenges. As such, you must be ready to listen to your client recount how he was hoodwinked into signing up for this certain web designer's scheme, or how much trouble he has had communicating and dealing with contractors, et cetera. It is your job to help your client look at his website issues one by one and to work out solutions for these issues.

5. **Help your client understand the audience of his website.** Many companies, especially those that are just starting out, do not really understand their audience. And because these businesses do not know and understand their audience, they cannot maximize the benefits their websites can bring, especially in terms of traffic and conversion. A website consultant functions to clarify this misconception to business owners and to identify what it is that the target audience really wants in order to create a website that attracts and engages audiences. Furthermore, you must make your clients realize that the website is not for them, but for their customers, which brings us to number six.

6. **Create user personas.** These are character sketches that represent the target audience of the website you are working on. This is an important step in web consulting, because the website is for the audience, and not for the website owners. A careful study of user personas should drive the design and development of the website. Before starting on coding and all things technical, make sure you have user personas down pat.

7. **Plan a strategy for the website.** As a website consultant, you know better than to plunge headlong into developing a website for a company without deciding on the strategy first. This includes having a dialogue with the website/ business owner and with the team that will put your recommendations and advice into action.

8. **Collect and analyse data from the website.** "Web analytics" "site statistics" "traffic data" "engagement metrics" these are just some of the terms anyone who owns a website must study, interpret and use in order to make their website perform well. However, not all website owners have knowledge of these numbers; neither do they have the patience or the time to learn about these things. This is why they hire a web consultant who can turn these data into actionable goals that will maximize the website and increase its return of investment.

Undoubtedly, the work of a website consultant is not limited to these eight items, but they make up the core of the tasks a web consultant must perform. A web consultant does not have to do the manual work such as coding or designing the website, but he will be responsible for coordinating the project and seeing its completion.

Often, a web consultant can be an expert in one field such as web design or marketing; he may be someone who works with other experts to fill separate roles needed in the development of one project. If you want to be a website consultant, you do not have to know everything about online marketing, programming, coding, SEO or data analytics. You must, however, have a working understanding of web and other online technologies. It also helps that you know different kind of web developers whom you can team up with to complete a project, or that you have the capacity for building relationships with such experts. Lastly, if you have already built a portfolio for yourself that you can show possible clients, then you just might be on the way to becoming a website consultant.

Taking the Idea to Market

The whole idea of being a website consultant is similar to being a project manager; even if you have only one of the skills listed above, you can still act as a website consultant if you have an eye for spotting good projects. That is, getting clients and pairing them up with a team that works on the website. How can you find such a team? By outsourcing on sites like Upwork. You can also call on various professionals from your network. Say, if you have worked with a certain web developer from the past, you might call on him again for a project that entails the kind of work he does.

Ready to launch yourself as the next website consultant? Here are some steps you can follow:

1. **Learn all you can about website consulting.** As mentioned earlier, you do not have to be a marketing expert, a web designer, a branding superstar or an SEO specialist in order to be a web consultant. But you must understand what each of these areas are, and how the team you are going to assemble will pitch in their knowledge and skills in order to make a unified website that will answer the demands of your would-be clients. You can read and do self-study over the internet, but you can also apply for online courses in order to build your knowledge and skills.

2. **Create a business plan.** Just like any other business, web consulting needs planning. Before you go telling everyone that you are now a web consultant, make sure that you understand everything about what you are aiming to do. What are your goals for the business? How will you achieve these goals? What kind of investments do you need to make? These are just some of the questions you must consider as you draft your business plan.

3. **Network.** Build a network of web designers, SEO experts, marketing specialists and other skilled professionals involved in website building and consulting. As your knowledge of website building and consulting increases, you can start building relationships. Create a blog where you can publish content about the things you learn, linking different websites and blogs. At the same time, be active in the web building and consulting scene online. Comment on blog posts, join forums and answer questions if you can. Join conferences and seminars online and offline. It might seem like a lot to do, but if you want to be a web consultant, you must not just know a lot about the business itself; you must also know the movers and shakers of the biz. From your network, you can even find someone who will mentor you and ease your way into web consulting.

4. **Build your portfolio.** Of course, it is natural that you start small. You can do this by offering your services free or for a small fee at

first, to people in your network. If your expertise is web design, you can work with a team of other experts as a web designer while learning the ins and outs of web consulting. Your previous work will be a good way of showing potential clients what you can do, and how you can help these potential clients reach their goals through their websites. Of course, you must continually update your portfolio for you will not be able to get clients if your portfolio is filled with old work. An updated portfolio will show potential clients how current and relevant your work is.

5. **Create your own website.** Perhaps the best way of showing potential clients what you can do for them is by having your own website. A website will not just help you make an online presence; it will also display and sell your knowledge, skills, experience, and the solutions that you offer your clients. It goes without saying that your website must be user-friendly and should communicate the kind of value hiring you as a web designer will give to your customers. You can use a free website builder like wix.com, or you can custom build your own website from scratch. Of course, there are advantages and disadvantages to both free and paid website builders, which is one of the most important things you need to consider as you create your website.

6. **Market yourself as a consultant.** If you have always been known in your network as a web designer, then make news. Contact former and existing clients and tell them that you are now offering web consulting services. Otherwise, no one will know of the new services you offer. Tell people what you offer as a website consultant, and how they can benefit from hiring your services.

7. **Eye the big companies.** While small and medium businesses are the ones that are most in need of website consulting, especially if they are just starting, it does not hurt to set your sights on larger companies. This is because bigger companies have a better understanding of why they need consulting in terms of their business. Not only that; when you bag a project with these big companies, the project will be an attractive part of your portfolio, and will encourage other companies to hire your services as well.

8. **Team up with high calibre experts.** From your networking days, you will surely have come upon experts that you work well with, or those who have really good output. Team up with these people in order to deliver what clients want. While you can always turn to outsourced help for every new project, it helps to work with people you trust, and people whose work is proven to be of high quality.

9. **Watch the competition.** What kind of services do other website consultants provide? What are their rates and how do they do business? This is especially needed when you are just starting, so you know exactly how to move with the market. Aside from being able to follow the trends, watching the competition also allows you to differentiate your offer, or to give potential clients more value.

10. **Keep learning.** The internet is always changing, as do trends and clients and their needs. As such, you must always keep yourself updated with the newest technology and the top trends in order to give your clients what they want and need.

Marketing the Idea

Once you have your website, your portfolio and the other things you need in place, you can start marketing your services. The following are some ways of spreading news about your web consulting business:

1. **Actively search for clients.** Go through different career and company websites and gauge which of these sites need some tweaking. Look for the webmaster of each site, or if there are no webmasters, search for marketing executives. Then, contact these webmasters or marketing personnel and give them your pitch. Be straightforward in your pitch, stating what you offer and how websites can benefit from hiring your services. Also include your rates and how your output justifies the amount you charge by stating what value they can get from consulting with you.

2. **Use your email listing.** Using your blog or website, offer your visitors something of value, such as tips to increase traffic, how to

write better content, or whatever it is that they could benefit from, in exchange for their email address. Use the email addresses that you would get to market the services you offer. You can even try offering low introductory rates to clients who sign up with you in a certain period. While not everyone you send an email to will hire you, it helps to make a lot of people know that you are offering website consulting services.

3. **Advertise on social media.** Almost everyone is now on social media. To get more leads and potential clients, you must also use social media. You can use Twitter, Facebook or even LinkedIn to spread content that will lead interested parties to your site. That said, you must make the content in your site easily shareable by adding widgets that allow visitors to post your content through single-click buttons for Facebook, Twitter, Pinterest, LinkedIn and Google+, among others.

4. **Create a brochure highlighting the services you offer.** You can send this brochure with your newsletter, or send a separate email and an invitation to try out your services. Alternatively, you can also print out this brochure, so you can hand it easily to people you meet, especially at conferences, seminars and other similar networking events.

5. **Use paid ads.** You can also make use of paid ads such as Google AdWords or Facebook advertising in order to increase your visibility online. While this might not be ideal for some start-up consulting businesses, it does not mean you will not benefit from it.

CHAPTER 9:

IDEA 9 – Internet Marketing Consultant

" The biggest risk is not taking any risk... In a world that changing really quickly, the only strategy that is guaranteed to fail is not taking risks"

-Mark Zuckerberg

Businesses left and right are going online, because let's face it; the internet is where most people are. Therefore, it is where the money is. Nowadays, having a website is not just an option - it is a requirement. However, just having a website is not enough. A company can have the best designed website that provides the best user experience and rich, attractive and engaging content, but if the business does not employ effective internet marketing techniques and strategies, the website will be a waste. Unless a business has an active online presence, it will not reach the goals it has set to achieve.

This is where an internet marketing consultant comes in. An internet marketing consultant will be able to provide the exposure a business needs in order for its website to gain traffic and to convert this traffic into revenue. These days, anyone with an internet connection and some knowledge on marketing techniques can easily set up an internet marketing consulting business. However, it takes more than just connectivity and access to some marketing strategies in order to succeed in this business. If you want to be an internet marketing consultant, you must possess these three characteristics, at the very least:

1. **High business proficiency.** Simply knowing the ins and outs of the internet is not enough. More than just internet know-how, you must have an extensive knowledge of the latest marketing techniques and possess business acumen that is based on real world experience. If you have a background in marketing and advertising, say, you used to work for a PR agency, then you will be a better consultant than someone who has just stepped out of school, even if that person is piled high with theories and strategies about advertising and marketing. Skills are transferable, so if you are a skilled marketer offline, chances are, you will do well to advise businesses about how to market their services online. Business acumen is also a highly desirable trait in internet marketing consultancy; the more you know about how to drive success in a business, the better you will be as a consultant

2. **Great interpersonal skills.** If you are a people person, you will be a good consultant. Like great sales people, consultants bank

on their ability to talk to people and convince them to take action. However, unlike sales people, consultants do not just push people through pitching. A great internet marketing consultant works with a client by carefully fleshing out ideas and solutions, and does not merely pitch to the client what needs to be done. People skills are also invaluable because they will help you network with a lot of experts that can help you provide more value to your clients.

3.   **Continuous development of knowledge and skills.** Internet marketing involves not just marketing skills, but also knowledge and proficiency in other areas such as industry trends, SEO, driving traffic and sales, technical know-how and other related concepts. A great consultant always keeps himself updated with the latest information and keeps learning about the current marketing strategies and techniques. Keeping yourself abreast with the latest trends and technologies will not just demonstrate professionalism; it will also help you bring more value for your clients, helping them achieve their business goals. Remember that the success of your clients is a reflection of your effectiveness as a consultant. The more clients you satisfy, the better your reputation becomes, which will attract more clients in the future.

Internet marketing involves a lot of areas. You can choose to focus on several areas or to provide full services across all these fields. Will you be a generalist or concentrate on a specialized niche? The choice is yours, of course. In order to make a decision, you must have a working knowledge of the following:

- **Market research.** This refers to the process of gathering data in order to determine if the product or service you are thinking of selling will sell. This involves examining your target market, identifying their needs and determining what added value you can put in what you have to offer. As such, market research also entails looking at similar products and services and how you can improve these services. Market research is done through questionnaires and polls, and through analysis of existing data and statistics.

- **Marketing plan preparation.** A marketing plan outlines a company's marketing and advertising activities for a period of time. Like a business plan, the marketing plan must have SMART (Specific, Measurable, Agreed Upon, Realistic Time-Based) objectives, which will direct the path the marketing campaign of the company will take. The plan must also include the target market, the current industry, the budget for the marketing campaign and the strategies that will be used in the campaign.
- **Search engine optimization (SEO).** SEO is one of the ways by which a website can rank higher in the search engine results. Through SEO, a website can have greater visibility, more visitors and hopefully, more conversions. SEO involves optimizing the content on the website so that search engines will list it on top of their results when people search for certain keywords, ideally those pertaining to the products or services the website offers.
- **Email Marketing.** This is a direct marketing tactic that pertains to sending electronic mail to target customers for the purpose of persuading these customers to take action: to buy a product, to subscribe to a service, or to download files.
- **Viral marketing.** This is a marketing strategy that makes use of social networks in promoting a product or service. The aim of this strategy is to spread awareness about the product or service through sharing in social media, much like the way a virus is spread, hence the term viral marketing. Viral marketing can be covert or direct, depending on the kind of strategy being used by the marketer.
- **Newsletter publishing.** Sending newsletters to an email list is another strategy businesses use to market their services. However, newsletters become more effective when they are not filled with attempts to sell; otherwise, the newsletter ends up in the spam folder, or the receiver chooses to unsubscribe to the newsletter.

If you want to be an internet marketing consultant, then you must be well-versed in these areas and other related fields. It is best to get some formal training, especially because there are a lot of conflicting strategies and information online. While you can choose to learn all the things you need to know on your own, it will help if you can follow a training program that will not just give you the knowledge and skills you would use as a consultant, but also help prevent errors you might make if you choose to do self-study. Being professionally trained can also help you get more clients because you have qualifications and certifications for show, unlike when you try to learn about marketing by yourself.

Example Ideas

After being fully trained in marketing trends and technologies, you can start promoting your services to different companies that need help with their marketing. The following are just some of the strategies you can offer your clients:

- **SEO.** Without a doubt, SEO still remains one of the best ways of marketing. These days, people are inundated with so much information, that they tend to ignore anything that is shoved in their faces. SEO works on the premise that it is the customer himself who seeks information. Say a person wants to find out the cure to eczema. He does a search on Google, Yahoo, Bing or other search engines. The search returns results and the customer clicks on the first few links, gets hooked on the information he reads and decides to buy the lotion that website offers. In order to get through all the noise and information, a website must rank high in the search results, which can be done by producing content optimized for search engines. Some business owners do not understand how SEO works, so it is your responsibility as an online marketing consultant to propose this strategy.

- **Facebook marketing.** Because almost everyone is on Facebook, not including it in your list of marketing methods is a disservice to your client. This social media network does not just make a business known to the online community; it also serves as a way of engaging followers and visitors and later turning them into paying customers.

Facebook can be used as a marketing tool in different ways: through Facebook groups, Facebook business pages and Facebook ads. Your job as a marketing consultant is to advise clients how they can maximize their use of Facebook to bring the results they want. Socialmediaexaminer.com offers these Facebook marketing strategies used by various businesses.

- **Pinterest marketing.** Pinterest has a total of over 150 million monthly users and is still counting. This number alone should send businesses scampering to make an account on Pinterest. Like Facebook, this social bookmarking site allows users to share content by pinning on different user-created boards. Unlike Facebook, Pinterest uses images and videos, which makes for a very visually pleasing experience. Copyblogger lists some ways to use Pinterest as a marketing tool.

- **Twitter Marketing.** Yet another effective way of putting out the word about a company is Twitter. With more than 300 million active users per month, an effective marketing strategy that makes use of Twitter will surely work to your client's advantage. Therefore, it is only logical that you direct and guide your clients into using Twitter to spread not just ads, but rather content that their target audience would be attracted to.

Taking the Idea to Market

Becoming an internet marketing consultant can be lucrative. After all, many people are now getting into business. While some entrepreneurs have a fairly good idea of marketing practices, not all new business owners are well-versed in making their products and services known. Therefore, they need the advice of internet marketing consultants.

Aside from the possible income, becoming an online marketer is challenging and fun, especially because it involves a lot of creativity and thorough and meticulous thinking. However, you cannot become an internet marketer just because you have decided it is the best home based business opportunity for you. Ready to become an online marketing consultant? Here are suggestions that can start you on your way to becoming an internet marketer:

1. **Train to become an internet marketing consultant.** Yes, you probably have a working background of marketing. You know the current trends and you understand how the market and the industry move. You could even be a naturally good marketer, like you were born for the job. But unless you get a break that will allow potential clients to see how good you are and how you deliver results, you probably will not get any clients. It is obvious that you will have competitors, and you would need to differentiate yourself from the others. If you have formal training and are fully certified as a marketer, you do not just have additional knowledge and skills; you also have qualifications to show potential clients. Digitalmarketer.com offers the best qualification and certification training programs for individuals interested in learning marketing.

2. **Find yourself a mentor.** Yes, you probably have been trained already and now possess certifications. However, you will get better experience and exposure to the online marketing business by being an apprentice to an internet marketing expert. You will not just learn more about the ins and outs of the biz; you also have a bigger chance of landing your first client with the help of your mentor.

3. **Build a portfolio.** As you play apprentice to your mentor, you can start applying what you are learning on the side. Volunteer to consult with non-profit organizations or humanitarian campaigns. You can also offer internet marketing consulting services at discounted prices. Start small, and then broaden your offer once you have found your footing.

4. **Build a website.** You are offering online marketing consultancy services, so it is only right that you create a website that will not just introduce you and your motivations, your talents and your skills, but will also showcase a portfolio of your past projects.

5. **Search for clients.** Use different marketing strategies to find clients to work for. Be creative. Market your wares the way you would help clients market their website, their products and their services.

Marketing the Idea

How will you find clients to consult? Here are some of the most common ways of marketing your internet marketing consulting services:

1. **Using your website (or your blog).** We have said this once, and we will say it again: write content that is attractive and engaging in order to increase traffic to your corner of the internet. By providing content (combined with your SEO efforts), you will naturally increase your ranking in the SERPs. The higher your ranking in the results, the more visible you become. The more visible you are, the more people you draw to your website. The more traffic you have, the higher the likelihood of reaching clients who want to hire your services.

2. **Google AdWords.** Of course, you need to market aggressively if you are to succeed as an online marketing consultant. Use Google AdWords in order to check for terms that clients that need advice on marketing are using when they search the internet. Use these and related terms when coming up with content and in putting up ads that feature your website and the kind of services you offer.

3. **Facebook marketing.** Of course you do not want to miss out on the big population of clients that you can find on social media, so use different social media networks like Facebook to market your services. Using the same premise of using content to attract and engage, you can set up a Facebook page that delivers helpful and valuable content without overpitching. Use techniques you have learned from your mentoring and pitching in order to convert your followers and audience into paying clients. While you are at it, leverage the power of using other social network sites as mentioned above: Twitter, Pinterest, Instagram and LinkedIn, among others.

4. **Local business advertising.** Regularly check local business job boards. Who knows, perhaps the client you are looking for is just a few blocks from where you are? You can also advertise your services. Use your network to spread word about your consulting services. Tell everyone you know that your services are for hire,

and ask them to refer you to clients who need some online marketing advice.

Succeeding as an Internet Marketing Consultant: Some Things to Consider

The road to success is not always smooth. As a beginner internet marketer, you probably have high hopes for your career. However, you will find soon enough that it is not as easy as you first thought. Like any other job, being an online marketing consultant requires hard work. You are probably inspired by success stories of internet marketers and how they are able to make money even without going through the daily 9-5 grind-inspiration is good, but know that there is no magic formula to being a marketing consultant. Your success, like in any other field, will depend on the kind of effort you put in. Here are some of the things you have to bear in mind:

1. **There are no shortcuts to success.** If it is not apparent to you yet, none of the home-based online business opportunities we have in this book are get-rich-quick schemes. Yes, you can make money from online consulting, but not quickly. You need to work hard, to persevere and to deliver results for your clients in order to grow your income exponentially.

2. **You do not need to be a whiz at coding, HTML and other similar stuff.** Yes, knowledge of these concepts is useful, but more than this or the ability to set up a website (which in any case you can outsource if you do not have the time, the energy and the patience for building one yourself), you need creativity, a keen eye for strategy and relationship-building skills that will see you through as an internet marketing consultant. The technical aspects can always be studied, but developing a real passion for what you do as a consultant is the more important part.

3. **Perseverance is key.** Just because you have a beautifully designed website that is chock-full of engaging content, it does not mean you will automatically have a lot of traffic and conversions. You need to sell yourself through your efforts and perseverance.

You never know when your first big break will come, the one that will propel your career as a marketing consultant, so you have to be persistent. While you are waiting for that opportunity, use the time to better yourself. Continue working on projects, even if they are small, and keep building your portfolio. Continue networking and providing value whenever you can. These efforts might go unnoticed at first; but bear in mind that in the long run, when you are finally successful, you will look back and see that it is these little things, put together will have made you the success that you are.

4. **Being an internet marketing consultant is not a one-man show.** Yes, you are probably very excited about making all things come together to bring you success, but be careful you do not suffer burn out in the process. Try not to take on too many projects at the same time. If you must take on a lot of work, then outsource some of the other tasks, especially those that are not under your umbrella of expertise. In addition, the people you work with, the outsourcers, can also be a part of your network and may refer some clients to you in the future.

5. **Competition is tough.** So you have to be tougher. Do not cower in the corner, afraid that the competition will eat you up. Instead, look at your competitors, see what they are good at, what they are doing right and the kind of success they are getting. You must also look at the not-so-good things the competitor is doing and think about how you can improve. Use this knowledge in order to bring more value for your clients.

CHAPTER 10:

IDEA 10 – Writing and Publishing Books on Amazon

"Whether you think you can, or you think you can't--you're right."

- Henry Ford

If you have always wanted to be a writer, then there is no better time for turning your dream into reality than now. In the past, getting a book published entailed a lot of work: writing the book, proofreading it, printing it out and sending copies to one publisher after another. If you were lucky, a publisher would take notice of your work and gamble on you. The book would get published and the publisher would market and advertise it for you. If your book was good, people would buy it and you would earn royalties for every copy bought. Otherwise, your manuscript would get tossed in the paper shredder, and your work would never see the light of day.

Thanks to technology, you are not limited to traditional publishing anymore, which follows the same tedious process. There are now e-books, which are the digital alternative to printed books. Through e-book writing, you can be the author you have always wanted to be without going through the harrowing ordeal of being rejected again and again. No more knocking at publishers' doors in order to get a chance at writing a book: now your book can be distributed and read by anyone, thanks to companies that offer self-publishing for authors, like Amazon and its Kindle Direct Publishing feature.

Why Amazon?

Amazon, the world's biggest online store that offers almost every product imaginable, and the Kindle, Amazon's signature e-reader, have changed the way people buy and read books. More importantly, they have given aspiring writers a chance to get published, and a break that they otherwise would not get through traditional publishing.

Publishing and selling your book on Amazon, gives the following benefits:

- **Quick, no-nonsense publishing.** In as little as five minutes, you can publish the book you have authored. Within 24-48 hours, people can start buying your book from Kindle stores located worldwide.
- **Your book, your rules.** Unlike in traditional publishing, you get to call the shots with regard to your book. You own the rights to your book and can make changes to it anytime you want; you can even change the book's list price.

- **More earnings.** You are entitled to up to 70% in royalty fees for every copy sold in countries like the USA, Australia, Canada, France, Japan, Italy, Spain, the UK, and more. You can also earn through the Kindle Owner's Lending Library if you sign up with KDP Select.
- **Digital and print publishing.** With Kindle Direct Publishing, you can publish e-books and paperbacks, free of charge.

Are you a frustrated writer? Your days of silently sulking are over. Whip out that laptop, start writing your book and take the first step to becoming a self-published author on Amazon.

Fiction or Non-Fiction: Which is which?

What should you write about? Many successful authors advise hopeful writers like you to write what you love. This advice is very helpful because if you are writing about something you do not give a hoot about, your output will most probably not sell because the writing does not come from the heart. This probably applies if you are writing fiction novels that belong in different genres: romance, adventure, and mystery, sci-fi, you name it. And if your aim in writing is to give voice to your creative side, then go ahead and write your dream novel. But understand that there are advantages and disadvantages to both fiction and non-fiction writing, some of which are listed below:

1. **Fiction endures.** There is something about fiction that draws readers, probably because everyone loves stories. Given the choice between fiction and non-fiction, people will almost always choose fiction, probably because fiction allows people to escape from today's realities and into a totally different world. Case in point is J.K. Rowling. Everybody knows Rowling wrote the series about the boy who lived, Harry Potter, and other companion books to the HP series. But not a lot are aware that Rowling also wrote -"Very Good Lives: The Fringe Benefits of Failure and the Importance of Imagination," a non-fiction book based on a commencement speech the author delivered at Harvard University.

2. **Non-fiction is practical and, therefore, more helpful.** Using the above-mentioned example, unless you are one of those impressionable types that pick up lessons from stories you read, then the HP series might not serve any purpose other than to entertain you -"Very Good Lives," on the other hand, is full of advice for new graduates, in terms of finding the good things about failure and the use of imagination to achieve success.

3. **Fiction allows you to find a distinct voice and style.** Famous writers are well regarded for the way they wrote and more often than not, they have written fiction, which aims to entertain and to elicit emotions. Non-fiction, on the other hand, is more direct, since the aim of non-fiction is to provide information and to spur the reader to action. There are, however, writers who are able to incorporate stories in their non-fiction works, and can somehow use their own voice even if they are writing non-fiction.

4. **Non-fiction requires facts.** Compared to fiction, which you can totally finish just by relying on your creativity alone, non-fiction requires discipline to write. You need to research and make sure that all your facts are correct. If you make a mistake writing non-fiction, you might lose credibility. If you make a lapse in the way your character develops in a novel, readers (fans, especially) can just chalk it up to a flaw the author can improve on in his next novel.

5. **Fiction writing can be lucrative.** This is true especially if you find a segment in the market that you can truly target and engage, such like the audience of Stephenie Meyer, author of the widely popular Twilight series, found. Despite the flack the series has gotten from critics with regard to the storyline and the type of writing, the Twilight books have still sold more than 100 million copies worldwide and have been turned into a film franchise, making Meyer one of the 100 world's most powerful celebrities in 2019, with an estimated net worth of $125 million. While many films have been based on non-fiction works, none of these films have made as much money as the Twilight series made.

6. **Non-fiction is easier to sell (at least nowadays).** More and more readers are slowly gravitating toward non-fiction. This can most probably be attributed to the increasing flow of information, thanks to the internet. The more people learn about things, the more they want to know about these things further. It can also be surmised that the work from home revolution is increasing the number of workers-turned-entrepreneurs. This has spurred the demand for information products (e-books, videos, podcasts, audiobooks, etc.) that will help the 9-5 worker transition into becoming a business owner.

7. **Non-fiction is easier to write.** Fiction writers can always fall back on the age-old reason for not writing: lack of inspiration. They can choose to do something else instead of writing, insistent on the fact that they can and will write when their muse finally comes to visit. Writers of non-fiction, more often than not, cannot use this excuse, since they are writing about facts – there is no need for inspiration, just thorough research. As such, it can be said that somehow, non-fiction writing is more productive, and not given to the whims of the writer.

The list goes on and on. We can present many points for both types of writing, but in the end, you will have to make the choice. What is it going to be for you? Take your pick.

Example Ideas

If you choose fiction, you can pretty much write anything you fancy. If you are a fan of Neil Gaiman or Terry Pratchett, then you most likely may be producing science fiction. You can follow Joyce Carol Oates' footsteps and write drama novels, or make like Rhys Bowen and write mystery novels. You can write young adult (YA) novels a la John Green, or you can choose to write children's stories, after famous writers like Eric Carle or Maurice Sendak.

If you think you would do better as a non-fiction writer, there are a lot of concepts you can explore. Of course, it helps that you genuinely know a thing or two about your topic and that you are very passionate about it.

Here are some ideas you might want to consider:

- **How-tos.** While there are many e-books available detailing procedures for doing things, this kind of e-book can still sell. Naturally, your topic must be highly in demand. Consider the topics of making money, building a business from scratch, health and fitness or even using home remedies to cure illnesses. The more in-demand the topic is, the more likely the book will sell.

- **Curated content.** People are ever hungry for information and they want to get their hands on everything in order to master something. However, not everyone has time on their hands. You would do them a great service by compiling and organizing facts and information about a certain topic and selling it in the form of a book.

- **Exposing little known facts.** You can also consider writing e-books that debunk myths. You can expose and correct misconceptions about health and fitness or dieting and exercise. You can also focus on insider secrets about a certain industry. For sure, this kind of e-book will sell.

A quick Google search can yield even more ideas, such as those you can find in contentbistro.com. As for the topics, you can use Google Keyword Planner Tool to search for the hottest topics that readers want to know more about. Analyze the data you get, and use it to decide on the topic for your book.

Taking the Idea to Market

Ready to launch your career as author? Here are suggested steps that can help:

1. **Decide on the topic and the audience.** Choose a topic that you are highly knowledgeable and interested in. After deciding on the topic, determine who your audience is. What does your target audience want? What do these people need? What kind of value can you give them through your book? These are just some of the questions that will guide you as you write your book.

2. **Write your book.** Of course, the book is the most important part of the venture, which is also one of the most difficult steps. You can take wisdom from "http://thoughtcatalog.com/cody-delistraty/2013/09/21-harsh-but-eye-opening-writing-tips-from-great-authors" like the ones mentioned above and others about the writing process. Brian Klems of The Writer's Digest offers suggestions for writing a non-fiction book. Paul Jun of Copyblogger has the following tips:

   - If you are on a Mac, use Pages. You can also use Microsoft Word. This way, the manuscript will be easier to format if you do the formatting yourself (more on formatting later).
   - Include the Table of Contents in your book.
   - Insert page breaks to eliminate blank pages after each section or chapter of the book. These blank pages can cause unnecessary annoyance for readers.
   - Do not use fancy fonts because Kindle does not recognize these fonts. Do not use headers or footers, either because it will mess up the final output.
   - Make sure to use italics and bold type for headings.
   - If you wish to include images in the book, use JPEG files.

   Alternatively, you can outsource the writing of the book through Upwork or other similar sites. If you go by the outsourcing route, make sure that you properly communicate the details you require to the outsourcer you hire.

3. **Proofread and edit your book.** When you are done writing your book, go over it again to check for errors in spelling, grammar, construction and punctuation. Better yet, outsource to someone else to check the book for you.

4. **Design your e-book cover.** Or commission someone to make it for you. Make sure that the cover is not just attractive, but also communicative of the value that readers will get from buying your book.

5. **Format your book.** Formatting your book requires know-how in HTML. If you have a working knowledge of this, you can follow

the simple formatting steps outlined by Amazon (check this on Amazon website). Otherwise, you can hire someone to do the formatting for you. You can specify that you want formatting for Kindle or epub (if you wish to sell your book through an additional platform outside of Amazon).

6. **Decide whether you will enrol your book in KDP Select or not.** KDP Select is a program for Kindle e-book authors. KDP Select offers the following benefits:

   - **Higher royalties**
   - **International publishing**
   - **Inclusion of your book in the Kindle Unlimited and the Kindle Owner's Lending Library (exclusive to Amazon Prime subscribers).** Kindle owners can "borrow" e-books free of charge, and the author earns some amount every time their e-book gets "borrowed."
   - **Two powerful promotional methods to choose from.** KDP Select offers kdp.amazon.com/en_US, which allows you to offer your book at a discounted price for a limited time. On the other hand, you can also opt to make use of the Free Book Promotion feature, which allows readers to download your book free for five days of your choosing. These five days must be within the 90-day period of enrolment within KDP Select.

     Note: Signing up for the KDP Select program binds your e-book to Amazon for 90 days. This means you cannot sell your e- book anywhere else. You can opt out of the program after the 90 days are up, and then sell the e-book through other platforms, but you will not be able to enjoy the promotional tools the system offers.

7. **Publish your e-book in Amazon.** This step requires a Kindle Direct Publishing account, which you can set up free of charge. If you wish to sell your e-book in paperback form, you can visit https://kdp.amazon.com/en_US/ to learn more about the process. You can go to www.acx.com if you wish to have an audiobook version of your creation.

Marketing the Idea

Uploading your e-book to Amazon is just the beginning - now you need to get the word out so people can learn about the book you are selling. Here are some ways to market your e-book:

1. **Build a fan base.** Even before you launch your e-book, make sure you have a website or a blog, at the very least. Produce blog posts related to the topic of your e-book. Again, you must determine your niche and your target audience, and write your content with these two in mind. Ensure that your content is attractive, engaging and provides great value for your target audience. Do not make any mention of your book just yet, but provide value for every piece of content you produce.

2. **Engage your target audience using social media.** Not everyone in your target audience will automatically know about your blog, so use different platforms that will direct people to your site. Use Facebook, Twitter, Instagram, Pinterest, Snapchat and LinkedIn to increase the visibility of your website. Again, it is important that you produce valuable content that will hook your target audience. Engage with your audience by replying to comments and direct messages.

   Promote your e-book through these channels, but make sure not to be in your audience's face all the time. Make sure you are still using a hook to attract attention and engagement, even as you post links that send visitors to your e-book landing page, where they can buy a copy.

3. **Network.** Using your blog, network with other authors in your niche. Write guest posts, or invite other authors to write guest posts on your own. This will attract more followers and fans for you. Join forums like Quora and other online communities. Ask questions and give your insights on topics in your niche.

4. **Build an email list.** Collect email addresses by providing something of value to people who visit your site. This could be tips, an infographic, an industry secret or a short e-book that is somehow related to your main product. They can get this freebie

by subscribing to your email list, after which they will be directed to a link that will allow them to download the freebie.

Use the email addresses you have gathered to send newsletters and updates to ensure that you continue engaging your audience.

5. **Use teasers.** With the above-mentioned platforms, create content that will serve as teasers for the launch of your e-book. If you have done your homework and have been actively engaging your audience, these teasers will heighten their excitement for the e-book, which can guarantee a lot of sales.

6. **Give your e-book away, free of charge.** Choose a select few to give your e-book to as a prize, or as a thank you for being a follower of your blog. Ask them to leave a review, and use these positive reviews as part of your e-book landing page.

7. **Use paid ads to target people who are most likely to buy your e-book.** Examples of these include Facebook Ads and Google AdWords. Remember to study first if direct advertising will benefit you in terms of ROI.

8. **Make use of the promotional tools in KDP Select (or not).** If it is your first time selling a book, then you can use the system to promote your e-book. These tools are also helpful if you have no other platform to sell your e-books on. Otherwise, you can opt out of this feature and use other promotional activities.

9. **Create an e-book trailer.** A short yet catchy video showcasing the value people will get from buying your e-book will create buzz, if properly shared through different social media channels. Post the video on YouTube and attach the link to your e-book landing page in the description box. You can also share the video in Facebook or tweet the link to increase visibility.

10. **Do not stop engaging your audience.** After the e-book has been launched, come up with effective ways to keep your audiences engaged. Ask for feedback or for suggestions about what your audience wants to see in your next blog post or probably the next e-book you will produce. Encourage questions. Post thought-provoking thoughts and comments to make sure that you are still current, even after your e-book has been launched.

CHAPTER 11:

IDEA 11 – Mobile Marketing Expert

"Many great ideas go unexecuted, and many great executioners are without ideas.

One without the other is worthless."

– Tim Blixseth

If you are new to the world of home based businesses, you are probably a little overwhelmed by words and phrases used by those that inhabit the work-from-home space. Perhaps you know Facebook, Twitter or Instagram; you most likely have a vague idea about how online advertising works - but mobile marketing? What is that?

Mobile Marketing Explained

Mobile marketing, in the simplest sense, refers to the kind of marketing done using mobile devices like smartphones, tablets and wearable gadgets. Because more and more people are using mobile devices, it is not just important, but also necessary, for businesses to make use of mobile marketing as part of their marketing strategy. In the age of the mobile device, mobile marketing is not just a buzzword; it is a critical tactic, especially because according to the latest Gallup poll, more than half of smartphone owners check their devices several times every hour.

To facilitate a better understanding of mobile marketing, it would be best to look at the different mobile marketing strategies:

- **Mobile Search.** Because almost everyone is on their mobile devices, it is only natural that they use their mobile devices to search for information and for things they want and need. Businesses take advantage of this by making sure that their respective websites are responsive; this means that the website automatically adjusts to fit the size of the screen it is being viewed on, be it the desktop, the laptop, the tablet or the smartphone.

- **Application based marketing.** This strategy makes use of mobile applications, which, according to the Deloitte Global Mobile Consumer Survey 2016 Report, have at least ten per cent more usage compared to mobile browsers. These include weather apps, social networking apps, and applications used for online banking, reading the news and music and video streaming. Through various mobile applications, marketers can target potential customers with in-app advertisements. A perfect example is how the Facebook application seamlessly integrates promoted ads so that users can barely see the difference between these ads and Facebook news.

- **Mobile pay. A research in 2018 by** www.gartner.com revealed that fifty per cent of consumers in mature markets used their mobile gadgets, that is, smartphones and wearable devices, to pay for their purchases. This is not surprising because it is easy and convenient. Businesses are taking advantage of this technological advancement by offering discounts and deals to customers that opt to use their mobile devices to pay for the products and services they offer.
- **In-game mobile marketing.** As the name implies, this kind of marketing tactic uses mobile games as a stage for showing ads. Since many smartphone and tablet owners are playing games on these devices, why not make use of these games to feature ads (especially for free games)? These ads could appear as video ads, banners ads or images that take up the full page or screen.
- **Video ads.** It goes without saying that there are now even more people watching videos, even television shows, on their mobile devices. Therefore, businesses would be wise to grab this opportunity and produce video ads. In today's world, people are not just more visual; they are also more driven inclined to watching video ads since carefully crafted video ads are more thought provoking and emotionally engaging. Well-executed video ads are a very effective means of getting people to buy products and services.
- **SMS (short message service).** While considered outdated (almost everyone has abandoned text messaging for a variety of instant messaging applications) by many marketers, some still swear by the power of SMS to draw in customers to their business. After obtaining the target audience's phone number, a business can send promos, discounts, markdowns and other deals straight to the customer's messaging inbox. Businesses can also make use of personalized news, offers and transactions, to target more customers.

Will you make a good mobile marketing consultant?

All the aforementioned strategies are very good ways of reaching a company's target audience, but the goal of marketing is not just to draw attention to the brand. The main aim of marketing is conversion, or getting the audience to act on the ad. When a viewer becomes interested in the advertisement, he clicks on the link included in the ad, which brings him to the product website. On the website he finds out more information about the product so he decides to buy. 'Ka-ching!' One sale, more money in the cash register.

A mobile marketer must have not just creativity, but a great understanding of different technologies, especially the trends that are at work, and the various ways of making these technologies work. A mobile marketer must also be able to know what to say, how to say it and when to say it in order to get customers' buy-in. This is the most critical part of marketing, which is why marketing, traditional or mobile is not for everybody. Therefore, a marketer is not just anyone who feels confident that he can make something look attractive enough to get a customer to buy it.

That said, anyone who wishes to be a mobile marketer must possess certain traits such as:

1. **Business savvy.** If you are going to turn mobile marketing into a career, then you must have at least the basic skills required of a businessman: oral and written communication, people skills, problem analysis, decision making, management, etc., are essential not only in your own business, but also in understanding where your clients are coming from. That said, you must also be able to visualize and communicate how the marketing strategies you propose would affect the different areas of the business of your client.

2. **Creativity.** In a world where everything come, changes and goes quickly, the ability to innovate is a must. However, there can be no innovation without creativity. You have to rise above what is commonplace to get your brand out there. If you are thinking of being a mobile marketing consultant, then you must also be

effective in teasing ideas out, looking at things in a different way and coming up with varied strategies.

3. **Storytelling abilities.** Seth Godin, a marketer, entrepreneur, speaker and author of several bestselling books says that all marketers are storytellers. In a world that is full of information, a business must be able to rise and make itself heard. How does it do that? Through storytelling. A good marketer, therefore, must be able to tell a compelling story that will not just move audiences, but will motivate these people to buy, to be consumers of the product or service the business offers.

4. **Digital know-how.** Come on, if you want to be a mobile marketer, then it is of course natural that you know how mobile marketing works. No, you do not need to know how to develop a website fully optimized for mobile devices or create an application, but you need to understand trends and data regarding various digital platforms used in mobile devices.

5. **Leadership skills.** Consultants are paid highly for their advice. If you want to be a consultant, then you must not just have good advice to give; you also need the skills to help you give advice. You must be able to sell yourself not just on account of the value of the advice you give, but also in the way you guide a business in achieving the goals you have set together. Thus, you should think and act like a leader, someone who would inspire, empower, and make things happen.

6. **A collaborative attitude.** Mobile marketing consultants should not just be natural leaders; they should also be people who understand how to work with a team and actually welcome collective action. As a consultant you need to be able to talk to many kinds of people and to accept ideas, no matter where they come from. This kind of attitude will not just make it easier for you to work with the clients who will hire you for your services; it will also help increase your creativity, since you pay attention to even the most far-flung ideas.

7. **Risk taking behavior.** If you do not like risks and are always on the lookout to avoid them, then becoming a mobile marketing

consultant is not going to be the best job for you. But this does not mean venturing blindly into the unknown, bringing with you your confidence as your only weapon. The most important commodity in the world right now is information. While there exists an abundant body of information especially now in the age of the internet, this information is too much for people already. This is why, as a marketing consultant, you need to continually get your ideas churning and taking bold yet calculated moves, especially when venturing forth and putting up something new for your clients. Only through incessant innovation, which requires great amounts of risk, will you be able to succeed as a marketer who actually gives clients the results they need.

8. **Proper judgment.** You know what they say: bad publicity is still publicity. But you cannot use that kind of logic in this case, especially because you are dealing with clients whose revenues hugely depend on how their products and services are being marketed. You must use proper judgment when it comes to the kind of tactics and strategies you will use for your clients. In the same way, if you take a misstep, own up to it. This is critical, especially because transparency is a very highly valued commodity now, more than ever. If you want to have staying power in this business, then you must have a good reputation. It goes without saying that you must believe in the clients you represent; be prepared to stand by them, or leave them, if their values clash with yours.

9. **A comprehensive view of different markets.** The internet has made it possible for anyone, regardless of wherever he is, to reach audiences from different places and to do business at a global scale. However, a website alone is not a guarantee of success. As a marketer, you must be able to distinguish the differences between and among markets, and use this knowledge to develop strategies to reach different kinds of audiences.

10. **Adaptability.** One thing to be said about today's market is that it keeps changing. This is why marketers must be versatile; they need to adapt to the ever-changing landscape of the market, the behavior of consumers, and the trends that come and go.

Taking the Idea to Market

Do you think you have what it takes to be a mobile marketing consultant? Then here are some steps to get you started in the home based business that is mobile marketing:

1. **Create a business plan.** A business plan is an important component in the creation of any business, no matter what the business is: manufacturing, logistics, or something as small scale as a home based business. Even if you plan to have a one-man consultancy, it is still essential to have a business plan, which is essential to give you direction. Without a carefully laid out plan, you will get lost. A business plan will not just guide your steps; it will also help you understand the business better, so you can set your goals properly and lay out what is needed to achieve these goals. A plan will also save you from taking missteps, and if ever there are mistakes, a look at your plan will help you decide which way to go, whether you take another tack or abandon the business for another one.

2. **Learn.** You cannot go to battle without your armor and gear, in the same way that you cannot build a business without knowing anything about it. While it is true that you do not really need a degree in marketing to be a successful marketer, having an education in mobile marketing is essential. You can choose to read up on all things that pertain to digital marketing, or you can sign up for mlearningsite.com, seminars and even one-on-one coaching programs. The first method is, of course, the cheaper of the two since you do not have to spend single cent learning about the biz. However, you need to spend a considerably longer time sifting through the wealth of information the internet has on mobile marketing.

   The second method, on the other hand, is relatively simpler – since paid courses are focused on concepts and insights you really need. Furthermore, these courses will eventually leave you with certificates that you can include in your portfolio. Of course, you will need some money to pay for these courses and programs, amounts that you could otherwise be using for other aspects of your business.

Whichever path you choose, be sure to make the most out of it. Learn as much as you can, and do not stop. Even when you start taking in projects, make sure that you are still picking up bits and pieces of learning that you can use in the future.

3. **Determine your niche.** Mobile marketing is a broad subject with many different components. There is email marketing, social media marketing, SMS, and all those other specifications. Which of these are you going to specialize in? Or would you rather be a generalist and have the ability to apply different tactics in your digital marketing campaigns? While it is good to be an expert in one or two fields, it also pays to have a general working knowledge of the other strategies. In the event that your campaign does not get the intended results using one strategy, you still have other tactics to fall back on.

4. **Build your online reputation.** If you are not known on the internet as an expert in mobile marketing, then you will not be able to get clients that will consult you for their marketing campaigns. This is why you must have a web presence that does not just show impressive information about you, your qualifications, certifications and a portfolio of past and related projects, but also content that demonstrates your knowledge not just in marketing strategies but also in understanding the market, its movements and its trends.

If you are not up to building a website just yet, you can start with blog writing. Through your blog you can publish content that will not just help businesses with their marketing efforts, but will also showcase your knowledge of the subject. Aside from regularly posting on your blog, you must also reach out to other people in the same niche, other bloggers who write about the same or other related content. You can visit these blogs, comment on them and interact with the blog writer and the other commenters. This way, you are putting the word out that you are someone who has knowledge on marketing. You can also write guest posts or invite other bloggers to write some posts for you.

You can also use social networking to make yourself known in Internet circles. While Facebook is said to be the most popular of all social networking sites, it is best for you as an online marketing consultant to have a visible presence on LinkedIn. You can post articles and content there, while networking with other digital marketers and consultants through joining groups and interacting with them.

5. **Grow your network.** Through your activities online, you can grow your network. You can get tips, suggestions and even brainstorm problems and solutions through your blog or social media accounts. However, you must not limit your ventures to online activities alone. You can also attend offline conferences, exchange business cards and contacts with the professionals you meet. You can also volunteer to speak for these seminars and gatherings, and earn some extra cash while you are at it. That said, you must not burn bridges, especially with those you have previously worked with. Although they might not have any business for you, they might refer you to some clients once you actually start your consultancy business.

6. **Build your website.** Once you have a lot of contacts already, you will most likely be prepared to build your own website. A website will establish your credibility and your renown as an expert in the online marketing world. As such, you must ensure that your website is professionally done, properly developed and checked for kinks, spelling and proofreading errors, design mishaps, usability issues and other glitches.

7. **Write a book.** You have your website. You have your blog. You have a fair amount of traffic to your website and your accounts. While these alone are enough, you would do better to get your name out there by writing a book. Pick a topic that you are very knowledgeable in and write about it in a book. This will add to your reputation, especially if you have authored a number of bestsellers already.

8. **Build your portfolio.** Start taking in work little by little. Ask friends for referrals, or you can look for startups on the Internet and start

pitching to them. Get an appointment to discuss with startup owners the benefits of consulting with you as a mobile marketer. Write your proposal letter, outlining your services and what you can do for the prospective client.

You can also try working as an apprentice first, or finding a mentor with whom you can do some projects. Not only will you learn skills and best practices from the mentorship; you will also get a feel of the entire consulting business and be introduced to some clients that you could work for in the future, or people who could refer you to new clients.

9. **Sell yourself.** With a portfolio of projects under your belt, you will be more confident in selling yourself as a mobile marketing consultant. You can use ads to direct prospective clients to your webpage so they can read more about the services you offer while you are generating traffic to your website using appealing content.

CHAPTER 12:

IDEA 12 – Selling Goods on eBay

"A pessimist sees the difficulty in every opportunity; an optimist sees the opportunity in every difficulty."

-Winston S. Churchill

If you are looking for yet another home based business idea, then why not try online retail? Basically, you find something to sell, post the item online with its description and price, together with your contact details. Someone who is looking for the item you sell sees your ad and contacts you. The item is sold and you get some extra cash.

Online buying and selling is gradually becoming the norm; even big brands like Jo Malone, Burberry, and Grenson have established their respective online stores to cater to customers who would rather make their purchases online. But you do not need to be a big name brand in order to sell items online. All you need are items to sell, some business savvy, and eBay.

Why eBay?

eBay is arguably the largest online marketplace in the world. Of course, some people would say that Amazon is the bigger and the better marketplace, and they may be right. However, if you are new to the online retail scene, it makes sense to start with eBay, for the following reasons:

1. **You can sell almost anything on eBay.** Do you have unnecessary clutter in the house due to stuff you no longer use? You can finally get rid of it while making extra cash when you sell it on eBay. This is one of the advantages of eBay, you do not need to have new and expensive merchandise in order to make some money, so you do not need big capital to start. But it is not just the sellers who benefit from this marketplace. People who are looking for unique, old or phased-out items find very good deals on the site.

2. **You do not need technical know-how.** If you want to go into the online retailing business, eBay can ease you into the buying and selling process without requiring you to build your own website or ecommerce store. All you need to do is to sign up on eBay, get a PayPal account and then you can start selling right away. You can learn about HTMLs and putting up your online retail store while you are earning, income that you would need to fund your online store if you decide that online retail really is the home based business for you, that is, selling stuff on eBay.

3. **You have the choice to put your item up for auction.** Unlike on Amazon where you have to sell your item for a fixed price, you can put your item up for auction in eBay. At the end of the auction period, the item gets sold to the highest bidder, which possibly means even more earnings for you.

4. **You do not have to spend a lot on marketing.** You do not have to spend a lot at all, when you choose to sell on eBay. The site generates its own traffic, and if there is a high demand for the product you are selling, then your listing can even rank high in the SERPs. And because of this traffic, you can have more people viewing your listing and a higher possibility of making a sale. No website? No worry!

5. **You can reach international customers.** eBay has a Global Shipping Program, which allows sellers to sell items to customers from other countries. All you have to do is get the item to the UK Shipping Centre and you are good to go. You do not have to worry about shipping the item to the country of destination.

If the above mentioned reasons are enough to get you to consider selling on eBay, then you should know how to go about the process. It is very helpful to know the ins and outs of every business venture you want to get into so you can avoid making mistakes.

How eBay Works

eBay is just like a garage sale, but online. There are many wonderful, unique and even bizarre finds on eBay, from Justin Timberlake's unfinished toast, to guinea pig armor, to the meaning of life. And then there are those regular things like video games, clothes, accessories, household items, and just about anything. If you are familiar with online buying and selling, eBay works just like that. However, the one difference with eBay is its auction function. Before it became the online marketplace that it is now known as, eBay was primarily an online auction site. Currently, items in eBay are sold in two ways:

1. **Through a fixed price.** Items that have a fixed price are sold as usual. You will know an item has a fixed price when it has a Buy It Now button included on the listing.

2. **Through auctioning.** Items that are for auction, on the other hand, are open to bidding for a fixed period of time (1, 3, 5, 7 or 10 days) depending on your limitations. When the time closes, the item gets automatically sold to the highest bidder.

An item can also be up for bidding and sold for a fixed price. If nobody buys the item by clicking the "Buy It Now" button, then the item will be sold to the highest bidder when the predetermined time is up.

As a seller, you can choose to put the item you are selling in an auction with a reserve, which is the minimum price that is needed to sell the item in auction. This price is hidden from everyone else, and only you, the seller know the price. Some sellers choose this option because they feel that a high start-bidding price will discourage bidders from placing their bids. Unless the reserve price is met, the item listing will continue to show the message "Reserve not met." Many sellers, however, do not use this option anymore because items with a reserve price are not always sold, and just start the auction at the lowest acceptable price.

Bidding on eBay

Unlike in traditional bidding where the winner is announced only after the highest bid has been entered, eBay bidding stops after a predetermined time regardless of the number of people still bidding on the item. Again, the highest bidder is supposed to buy the item because the bid is considered a contract. If the item is not paid for, it gets recorded in the buyer's account. Unpaid items on an account can cause account suspension; the user might also be restricted from buying or selling on eBay.

Some bidders use the automatic bidding system, which allows them to stay on top of the bidding, provided that they bid the highest amount. Also called max bidding, this system bids on behalf of the owner who bids the maximum amount. To illustrate, let us use this example:

Goldie has put up a chair for auction on eBay, for three-day duration. The minimum starting bid is $5.00.

Cindy sees the listing and because she likes the chair a lot, she bids $15.00 on it using the max bidding system. Goldie, the seller, and the other bidders on the item do not know of this amount. What eBay does is it bids $5.00 on behalf of Cindy, and then raises the minimum bid to $5.25 (starting bid plus one increment).

Jake sees the chair and bids $5.25. Because Cindy still has the highest bid of $15.00, eBay automatically bids $5.50 on her behalf, raising the minimum bid to $5.75. Jake tries again and bids $6.00, only to be outbid by Cindy's $6.25, using the automatic bidding system.

Aurora sees the listing for the chair and bids $18.00 using the automatic system. This then raises the current minimum bid to $15.25, which was Cindy's original bid, plus one increment. Aurora is now the highest bidder, so eBay then bids $15.50 for her. Cindy bids $16.00, and eBay again bids $16.25 on Aurora's behalf. The bidding period ends, and the item is sold to Aurora for $16.25, even though she originally bid $18.00 for the item. Aurora then sends the amount to Goldie through PayPal. Goldie then prepares the chair and ships it to Aurora.

Preparing to sell on eBay

One man's trash is another man's treasure, so they say. Maybe you have a lot of items lying around in the house that you can make some money out of. But hold your horses; before selling on eBay, you must first do the following:

1. **Decide on the kind of eBay account you will open.** Are you starting with a personal account or a business account? Before you decide, you will naturally need to know the difference between the two. Basically, a personal account is mainly for selling a few items here and there whenever you feel like it – sort of like a hobby, or something you wish to do from time to time. A business account, on the other hand, allows you to sell many goods regularly, or to resell items that you have bought for a profit. If you already have an online or a physical store, it is advisable to create a business account. If you are just testing the waters, then you can keep it simple and set up a personal account at first. You can

later change your personal account to a business account, once the business is in full swing. It goes without saying that you must learn all there is to know about registering your eBay business name, the corresponding taxes and other laws about starting a business.

2. **Register for a PayPal account.** Yes, eBay has other payment methods aside from PayPal like bank-to-bank transfers, money order, checks and other online payment services but these methods are limited to only a few item categories. For everything else, eBay requires PayPal to ensure buyer and seller protection. One thing you must know is that PayPal will charge you a fee for every transaction. Currently, seller fees are 3.4% of the amount of the item being sold and the shipping fee, plus handling fee. The fees can be higher if you are selling the item internationally. Because figuring out the fees can be confusing, some people opt to use fee calculators. To be able to use all the benefits of PayPal and to buy and sell without the hassle, make sure your account is verified by linking a bank account to it.

Keep in mind that these fees are part of your expenses as a business and must be factored out when calculating your profits and your taxes as well. Again, you must decide if you will be setting up a personal PayPal account, which will bear your real name, or a business account with your business name. You can keep two PayPal accounts, one personal and one business, or you can choose to upgrade your account from personal to business, as you would your eBay account, should you decide that an eBay selling business is for you.

3. **Learn about eBay fees.** If you make a sale, understand that you will not get all the money from the transaction, you have to pay the PayPal fee, the shipping costs and eBay fees. Not having a brick and mortar store does not mean that you will be free from expenses. Basically, eBay charges you fees on your subscription (if you will be listing 50 or more items monthly), insertion fees, final value fees and fees for features you might want to avail yourself of. The different fees sellers pay can be found on the eBay site.

4. **Be ready with shipping supplies for the items you are selling.**
When you list an item on eBay, you will be required to declare the weight and the dimensions of the box the item will be packed in. Make sure that you have weighed and measured the item properly before even listing it. This will ensure that you do not have to pay extra shipping costs if the item turns out to be bigger and heavier than the measurements from your guesswork; it would be unfair to charge the buyer more for shipping, if you already have declared in your listing how much the shipping fees are.

5. **Calculate how much profit you will get for every listing.** As previously mentioned, you will have to consider the different fees that have to be taken out from the sale you will make. So even if eBay advises you to start your auction at $.99, you might want to set a minimum opening bid that will allow you to gain some profit. Or you can skip listing your item as an auction and sell it as normal using the "Buy It Now" option. Once you have gotten the hang of selling, you can try using the other selling features such as the setting a reserve feature or the "Make an Offer" feature.

Taking the Idea to Market

Still reading? Then you are probably really convinced that eBay selling will be a lucrative home based business opportunity. Here are the steps to get you started:

1. **Create your eBay and PayPal accounts.** The previous section provided you with an explanation on the importance of these accounts. Again, if you are starting from scratch, it is best to start with a personal account and then upgrade later on.
A note on creating your eBay account: As much as possible, use a professional sounding email address and username. Your username will appear in your account and will be used to identify you, so you do not want a username that is obscene, profane or suggestive. You might want to think of a reputable name, or something catchy that will make it easy for buyers to remember you. If you are thinking of selling items under a single category,

you might want to think of a username related to the category for easy recall. While you can change your username once every 30 days, it is not advisable, because some users who might be looking for you will not find you. This can result in lost sales.

2. **Be an eBay buyer.** You need to do this for two reasons:

(1) To familiarize yourself with how eBay as an e-commerce platform works. You will gain more insight into the psychology of selling if you first become a buyer. By putting yourself in a buyer's shoes, you will have more understanding about how eBay buyers think, so you can adjust your pricing, your shipping options and even the way you will do customer service as a seller.

(2) To get feedback. Feedback is important, especially for new sellers. You cannot expect buyers to start bidding on or buying your items if they do not see any feedback on your account. To get feedback, you can buy items sold for $0.99, with free shipping. These are items that you can use as a seller: bubble wrap, packaging tape, boxes and similar materials, or books that you can use to learn more about the business you are planning to start. After making the purchase, leave positive feedback for the seller, and send him or her an email asking for feedback on your account. Sometimes you can automatically get feedback even without asking for it.

3. **Prepare to list the items you want to sell.** Make sure that you have upgraded your eBay account to a seller's account; otherwise, you will not be able to sell anything. Before you put your items up on eBay's listing, here are some things you need to do:

   • **Research the value of the item you are listing.** Since you are new to selling, you do not know how much to list your item for. You can use www.terapeak.com to find popular products on eBay, to see how sales are moving for certain items, and to determine how much you can sell your item for. You can also use the Advanced Search link on the upper right corner of the page to look at how much items such as yours are being sold for.

- **Choose a good title for your listing.** The title alone should capture buyers' attention, so make sure that it includes the brand and a specific description of the item. It would be best to include the color, the dimensions, model number and even the condition of the item. Of course, it goes without saying that you should use the correct spelling, even if you do not need to be grammatically correct (it's a title, not your high school essay).

- **Write a clear description of the item.** Include all the details buyers need to know about the item: the model, color, size, country of origin, brand/maker, date of manufacturing and other similar specifics. State the condition of the item, and make sure that you include flaws or even repairs done to the item. You do not want to mislead your buyers, so do not embellish, although you can include a story that will appeal to the buyer.

- **Use high quality images for your listing.** Potential buyers want to see how the item look, so make sure that you include actual photos of the product in your listing. This is most especially needed if you are selling something that is not brand new. If there are some scratches or dents on the item, take a photo of that, too. Use good lighting and do not use any filters because you want to show buyers the item as it is, kinks and all.

- **Determine how much profit you want to make from selling the item.** Bear in mind that selling on eBay is not a get-rich quick scheme, although there have been some lucky sellers who have been able to sell a single item for tens of thousands of dollars or pounds or more. Use your research to put a price on the item, and be sure to take out the fees when you calculate for the amount.

4. **List your item.** Use the above mentioned tips to come up with a listing that will attract attention and, more importantly, buyers who will bid on or buy the item. Of course, you need to decide whether you will put the item up for auction, sell it, or put it up on auction with a "Buy It Now" option.

5. **Ship your item to the buyer.** Once a buyer sends you the payment, you can ship the item. Make sure that the item is properly packed and that it has the correct address.

6. **Lather, rinse and repeat.** With the profit you will get from your first few sales, you will be able to start buying items that you can sell (of course, you need to use Terapeak, the up and coming alternative tradu.io, or Google Keyword Tool to determine which items are in demand and will sell for good prices) on eBay. You can find such items in eBay, in e-commerce stores from different places, or local charity shops, or even in live auctions held in your place.

CHAPTER 13:

IDEA 13 – Local Business Consultant

"Whatever the mind can conceive and believe, the mind can achieve."

– Dr. Napoleon Hill

Do you want to give up your 9-5 job for something that is not as difficult, as stressful or as dragging as the daily grind inside the cold or hot, square cubicle of your grey corporate world but you do not have the drive or the inclination to sit in front of the computer and be an internet worker? Are you having a tough time trying to reconcile the skillset you have developed over the years in the office with the requirements of an online job? Worry not; you can get away from your day job and still be able to do something that puts food on the table: local business consulting.

Business Consulting: What's the Buzz?

If you have been in the corporate world long enough, then you will know that consulting is a valuable part of any business. Even if you are not the boss, you likely have been in a meeting with your manager or supervisor telling everyone that the company is hiring a new consultant. You probably know that a consultant is someone who comes in and offers solutions to the pain points your company faces. But is that all there is to business consulting? What is business consulting? What do business consultants do?

Merriam-Webster defines consulting as the act of "providing professional or expert advice," and a consultant as "one who gives professional advice or services." These are very broad definitions that lead us to the question, can anyone who is an expert in his or her own field become a consultant? The answer is both yes and no.

Yes, you can be a consultant if you are knowledgeable in fields that businesses require. If you are a whiz at computers, their peripherals and technology in general, you can be an IT consultant. If you are well-versed at sales after all those years of working in company sales departments, you can get a job as a sales consultant. If your forte is in marketing and advertising, you can sell yourself as a marketing consultant to businesses that need to learn a thing or two about how to make their marketing strategies better.

However, because you have the knowledge does not necessarily mean that you will make a good consultant. You also need the skills, the aptitude and the attitude that the job requires. Unless you have the passion and the aptitude for consulting, you will probably end up frustrated and disappointed, not to mention broke.

Do You Have What it takes to be a Consultant?

Before you hand in your letter of resignation and announce to the world that you are leaving your current position to become a local business consultant, you must first examine yourself. Take a long, hard look at your talents, your motivations and your preferences and answer the following questions as truthfully as you can:

1. **Are you ready to start a local consulting business?** Being prepared to enter a new business, any business, entails a lot of things. If you are going to start a consulting business, you must know and understand the ins and outs of the business, not just the kind of work you will be doing. Aside from the knowledge and skills that are required in your field of expertise, you must also have the maturity to take on different tasks, especially if you will go it alone. To help you assess your readiness, you can make a checklist that includes the following items (as you think your decision through, you might come up with other things you need to be ready with, physically, emotionally and financially):

   - **Certifications, qualifications and licenses.** Of course, you will need certifications that will show your qualifications as a local business consultant. Having such documentations will help give you a solid reputation that will get the trust of clients and your other prospects.

     It is of the utmost importance that you start off on the right footing by registering your business. Will you be registering as a sole owner, an LLC or a partnership? Naturally, you need to learn a lot about these aspects of the business, so you must read a lot, www.usa.gov/business and www.gov.uk/browse/business is a good place to start.

   - **Finances.** What is your financial standing? Do you have money saved to fend for the time you are out of work? Establishing yourself as a local business consultant will take time, so you must be prepared for a lull in your cash flow, especially in the beginning. And while starting a consulting business will not have overheads as big as opening a retail store, you will still need money to start.

- **A business plan.** You can never start a good business without a solid business plan. A well-written plan will outline your goals for the business, and the steps you need to take to achieve these goals.

- **Mental and emotional stamina.** Will you be able to take on all the tasks that your startup consulting business will require? Do you have the patience, determination and daring to push forward with the decision to become a local business consultant? Are you attentive, creative and innovative? Are you organized, resourceful and thorough? You do not just need know-how in the field you choose; you must also possess the right mindset and attitude toward the business and your tasks as a consultant. These are especially important because you will find that some aspects of the business are not really part of your expertise. For example, you may be really good when it comes to working with people and coaching, but marketing may not be one of your strengths; in that case, how will you be able to get clients to hire you?

2. **Are you willing to do what it takes to see your local consulting business through?** As owner of the business, you will not just do consulting, you will be wearing different hats and performing different functions, such as:

   - **Marketer and promoter.** Simply put, if you cannot get clients, then you cannot have a business. As marketing or advertising manager, you need to come up with a strategy for marketing your offering, be it through online marketing, print and media ads, or word-of-mouth referral.

   - **Client relations officer.** Aside from being a consultant, you must also build relationships with your clients. This entails making sure that they are satisfied with your services. You do not only make your clients happy; you also open doors for repeat business in the future.

- **Admin executive.** You will be your own secretary: answering phone calls, setting appointments and schedules, updating records, and other similar tasks. Unless you get someone else to man your "office" for you, you will have to shoulder all these responsibilities.

- **Collections officer.** You also need someone to take care of billing and collections. Again, if you do not have a dedicated person to do this, you have to undertake this responsibility as well.

- **Bookkeeper or accountant.** Running a business involves money coming in and going out. In order to keep your records in order, you need to account for the movement of your finances. This is important not just to see how profitable the business is, but also to make sure that the business is not losing money and that all your taxes and required fees are being paid.

- **HR manager.** Unless you already have someone in place to fill up this role, you will also need to act as personnel manager, especially when you start expanding and taking in employees to fill different roles in the company.

3. **Are you confident in your ability to perform all the responsibilities a local consulting business entails?** Readiness and willingness alone are not enough; you must have the ability to deliver high quality consulting services while making sure that all the other aspects of the business are running smoothly.

   As a consultant, you will be handling various tasks, including:

   - **Being the expert that you are.** If you have a reputation for being a marketing guru that brings increase in ROI, then chances are, businesses will hire you on the basis of your reputation alone. Once businesses in your locality get wind of how good you are, they will be making a beeline for your services.

   - **Problem identification.** Sometimes, a company knows that something is wrong with its system, but cannot identify what the issue is. Therefore it needs an outsider like you who can look at the system without biases to diagnose the problem.

- **Bring forth necessary change.** A company with close-knit employees might find it difficult to effect change without offending anyone. You could be hired to start the change; since you are not part of the company and its culture, you do not have to worry about pleasing anyone, so you can initiate the change and get everyone else to follow. You can be also called upon to fire employees or discipline an entire team: something managers or supervisors find hard to do.
- **Teach, coach and up train.** If there are new skills employees in a company need to learn, your expertise might come in handy. If you have new sales tactics to teach, you could be hired to up train sales employees of a local business, or you could coach the marketing division about groundbreaking marketing strategies.
- **Create a new product, service or a new business altogether.** If you are a creative and innovative consultant, you could be hired to spearhead a project that will create a new product or service. If you are an expert in creating business streams, you could also be hired to deliver such services for a local business.

If you answer "yes" to these three questions, then being a local business consultant might just be the home based opportunity you have been looking and waiting for. If so, read on for more information.

Example Ideas

A consultant can be an expert in almost any field, but according to www. entrepreneur.com/article/41384, the consultants in the following fields of specialization are in particular demand these days:

1. **Business.** Is business acumen one of your strongest suits? Are you able to look objectively at a situation and gather insights about it? Can you easily come up with various options in solving an issue? Do you do a good job of coming up with a course of action to reach goals? Then you can use your business smarts in helping businesses around you grow and prosper.

2. **Accounting.** Did you graduate with a degree in accounting? Are you a certified accountant? If you are through working with just one company, you can branch out and do consulting for different businesses in your locality. Since every business needs someone to take care of their books, you have a lot of opportunity to succeed as an accounting consultant.

3. **Auditing.** If you are well-versed in reviewing financial reports, risk assessment and strategic operations, then you could be in for a lucrative position as an auditing consultant because businesses both large and small need help with these areas.

4. **Marketing and advertising.** Because there are many competing businesses, companies are always on the lookout for great marketing campaigns and awesome rock star marketing and advertising consultants that will help them get ahead. If coming up with amazing advertising and marketing campaigns is your cup of tea, you will surely get a lot of clients to hire you.

5. **Internal and external communication.** Believe it or not, many businesses fail to achieve their goals due to a lack of communication initiatives. Enter communication consultants, who help organizations move towards the achievement of their objectives through internal and external communication strategies.

6. **Computer and IT.** Many startup businesses are spearheaded by go it alone entrepreneurs. As such, they do not always have technological capabilities. If you are an expert on the internet, software and hardware, you may find that being a computer and IT consultant can be a profitable endeavor.

7. **Recruitment.** If your heart is in recruitment and you find that staying in one company as a headhunter can get pretty boring because the company does not have a high churn, you can quit that job and be a headhunting consultant instead. This way, you can hop from one business to another, helping them with their recruitment. You get to do the job that you love while helping different organizations find the kind of employees they need.

8. **Career.** Millennials have a high churn in the workplace, brought about by their continuous searching for growth and development. As such, career consultants have become very much in demand, as they guide their clients toward career choices that will bring in not just the big bucks but also job satisfaction.

9. **Tax.** As long as there are taxes to be filed, tax consultants will never go hungry. And because there are a lot of up–and-coming businesses, tax consultants will have a lot of clients to go around.

10. **Publishing.** Consultants who are well-versed in publishing can help both big and small businesses in the locality launch magazines, newsletters and even websites as part of their marketing strategy.

Taking the Idea to Market

Ready to take on the local business arena by storm? Here are some steps you can follow:

1. **Decide on your niche.** What kind of consulting do you want to do? Do you excel in marketing, accounting or business management? What expertise do you have to offer your prospective clients? It would also help to survey the businesses in your area to see what kind of help they need, and what kind of consulting these businesses could benefit from.

2. **Build your expertise and your skillset.** You cannot give what you do not have, so make sure that you have the qualifications that are needed in a consultant. If your expertise matches the needs of the businesses in your locality, that is all well and good, but this does not mean you should stop learning additional skills that you could use to further your career as a consultant. If the demand does not match your field of specialization, then you need to exert more effort. Get some training, enter certification programs and educate yourself about businesses and their needs. It also helps to have certifications to show, proof that you know exactly what you are doing, to get your clients' trust and buy-in.

3. **Find a mentor.** As you study and learn about consulting in general and the niche you want to specialize in, you will come across

a great many people in the consulting community, both online and offline. You will undoubtedly read blogs and online articles written by other consultants, and from here you will learn a lot of insights and concepts that you can use when you finally start consulting. You will also be attending conferences and seminars, where you will be meeting even more consultants and experts. It is only natural to network with these people, and belong in a community of consultants. But more than just networking, you should endeavour to find yourself a mentor, someone who would show you the ropes. Find yourself a successful consultant, and offer some of your services, say, if SEO writing is one of your stronger suits, you can offer to write blogs for him, or help out on one of his projects. Who knows, this mentor might even help you land your first client!

4. **Create your business plan.** You are going to build a business, so it is wise to write down how you plan to go about creating the business. What are your objectives for your consulting business? What resources do you need to achieve your goals and which steps will you take toward the success of your business? It also helps to put down on paper all the details of the business, including the kind of services you will offer prospective clients. Putting down everything in writing will help you see the kind of work you need to do to achieve your business goals.

5. **Be a thought leader in your locality.** Just as you would online through your blog or your website, you need to sell yourself as a professional who knows exactly what he is doing, and can make success happen for businesses in your area. To do this, you can create a magazine or a newsletter containing news, tips and features focused on businesses in your area, and how they can increase their visibility, or how they can improve their marketing strategy, etc. You can publish this online, or if you have the budget, print it and demonstrate it periodically. This will help establish your name as an expert, someone businesses can turn to for help.

6. **Find clients.** Without a client to serve, you will not be a successful consultant. Therefore, you need to really sell yourself. Aside from

publishing your magazine or newsletter, building a website and a blog and publishing all these helpful content for local businesses, you also need to be aggressive in finding clients. You can do these through:

- **Brochures.** These will help familiarize your services to the businesses in your area. Make sure that your brochure includes some information about you, the kind of services you offer, why businesses should hire you, and even a sampling of companies you already have done business with.

- **Cold calling.** Many businesses do not think they have a problem until it is looking at them square in the face. They will not know until you tell them that you can make their businesses better, their revenues bigger, and their systems more efficient. When you do cold calling, make sure that you prepare your pitch beforehand. Anticipate questions and problems and present these in a short but persuasive sales pitch.

- **Advertising.** You can also look into paid advertising, aside from doing the usual blogging and content writing in your website. You might want to have ads shown on local television or aired on the local radio.

- **Speaking at conferences and seminars.** Network with the movers and shakers of your community and be in the know about upcoming seminars. Offer to speak on a topic you have a great knowledge of so business owners can see you as an authority on the subject. This is also a great way of getting clients.

CHAPTER 14:

IDEA 14 – App Designer

"I'm convinced that about half of what separates the successful entrepreneurs from the non-successful ones is pure perseverance."

- Steve Jobs

Apps are all the rage these days – scratch that; they have gone past being a trend, and are now a staple in the daily life of every mobile gadget owner. And because of the increasing number of mobile gadget users, there also has been a steady rise of apps available both in Google Play (more than 2.2 million apps) and the Apple App Store (almost 2 million apps).

CACI Ltd, data experts, in the UK Metro Newspaper of July 1, 2019 expect the proportion of customers using banking apps to reach 71 per cent by 2024 in UK compare to 55 percent going into their local branch. In other words, more people will soon use mobile banking than visit high street bank branches. One can argue that this is almost universal in the developed and the developing world.

When smartphones and other mobile devices came into being, no one knew that mobile applications, or apps, as everyone wants to call them, would reach this kind of popularity. The November 2016 Ericsson Mobility Report predicted that there will be 6.1 billion smartphone users worldwide by 2020, which means that app popularity will continue to soar. Businesses wishing to take advantage of this predicted trend must then offer additional services through apps, in order to meet the rising mobile demands.

Mobile Applications: What's About Apps?

What is an app? Basically, an app is a standalone program that aims to give mobile users a simpler and more convenient way of doing things. Take for example the eBay app (available in both Google Play and the Apple App Store). Users can access the website on their browsers, but they still download the app because it is optimized for mobile use. Because the app is made specifically for mobile devices, users find the content more appealing, not just in design but also in functionality. Just by tapping the eBay icon on his device, a user can easily access the app and browse products he or she wants to buy. A seller can even list an item he wants to sell, in just a few taps.

The popularity of apps is unmistakable; there are gaming apps, productivity apps, entertainment apps and even dating apps – you name it. As the Apple tagline goes, "There's an app for that." But what is it about apps that people find so great? Aside from being user-friendly, what edge do apps have over the mobile browser? Here are several points:

1. **Added features.** Most apps offer more features. For example, e-commerce apps give discounts and other deals exclusively for app users. Apps are also able to access the smartphone's sensors or camera, something mobile websites cannot do.

2. **Speed.** With apps, users do not need to log in all the time, entering passwords and wasting precious time. There is no need to type web addresses, either. A user just has to locate the app, tap on it and ta-da! What he needs is right there on the screen. Need we say more?

3. **Notifications.** Apps give users notifications so they do not miss out on important things. Unlike mobile browsers, apps can generally integrate into the operating system of the mobile device.

4. **Security.** Users generally feel safer buying through an app over buying over a mobile browser, especially now when fraud and identity hacking are widespread.

5. **Ownership.** Users feel that they have more power and control over an app. After all, it is the user who downloads or deletes an app as he pleases; there is no such feeling with websites and web browsers.

6. **Cool factor.** Many users feel that the more apps they have on their smartphones, the "cooler" they are. In a way, people have gotten addicted to apps, which explain why everyone just has to try the newest apps in the market.

7. **Greater functionality.** With apps, anyone with smartphone can be a MacGyver of sorts. (en.wikipedia.org/wiki/MacGyver) A mobile device can transform into a document writer, a cloud storage device, a retail store, an e-book reader, a newspaper/ magazine, a recipe book, a pastime, a flashlight, a calculator – its uses are virtually endless, with different apps.

8. **Neat packaging.** Successful apps have an attractive interface; otherwise, they get buried in the pile of the forgotten apps. A great app looks good and feels great to use.

9. **Practical.** There are scores of free apps that users can download, but even if a user has to pay for a desired app, he does not need to shell out more than $10.00 for it, as most apps cost as low as $0.99. People typically do not want to miss out on such a great offer.

10. **Adaptable.** Apps continue improving, with regular updates that app developers release. Whatever issues users encounter with the app can be refined to reach user satisfaction.

Today's Businesses and Mobile Applications

Apps are not popular just because of mobile users; they have also been made popular by different businesses that utilize apps for the following reasons:

1. **Apps make businesses more visible.** An app makes it possible for users to see the brand all the time, even if the users themselves do not notice it. Supposing you have an e-commerce store. While a customer with your app on his phone does not buy from your store every day, the simple fact that he can see your app icon is enough to keep you fresh in his eyes. The next time he needs to make a purchase, he will not think twice about buying from you, you could become his go to e-retailer.

2. **Apps are a good marketing strategy.** Through apps, a business can deliver information to its consumers immediately. This information includes new products, additional services, discounts and other offers. The more informed users and consumers are, the more likely they are to buy products and use services.

3. **Apps allow businesses to give added value to customers.** Businesses need to differentiate themselves from the competition, and one way of doing this is by providing their customers more value. Through apps, businesses can offer loyalty programs without the need for those plastic point collection cards. All the

customers need to do is to bring out their phones (which they have with them all the time) and access the app every time they make a purchase. Loyalty programs and other value-added programs do not only increase customer engagement; they also help increase ROI.

4. **Apps enhance customer service.** An app can help customers access a business' services any time they want or need to. This is most especially important for businesses that do not offer customer support 24/7. It can get awfully frustrating for customers to not have an open line of communication during urgent times, so an app that helps them connect with the business can help ease their mind.

How Apps Make Money

Sure, we have established the "hows" and the "whys" behind the popularity of the mobile app. But these still do not explain how apps can earn you money, should you decide to be an app designer or developer. If you do not believe designing an app can put food on the table, you are not alone. After all, most apps are inexpensive, and many are free. So how come people keep developing apps? Here are some ways apps earn revenue:

1. **In-app purchases(IAPs).** You are probably familiar with IAPs, which come with free apps. The premise is that you download the app free of charge, and then later pay for the full version of the app, or for additional features. This method works because it allows users to download the app so they can try it first. If they like the app, then they pay for the full version. If they do not, they delete the app.

   Apps with in-app purchases are called freemium apps. The beauty of these apps lies in the fact that they eliminate the difficulty of deciding whether to download or not. People are naturally wary of paying for something they are not sure they would find useful or enjoyable, so freemium apps sort of give them a trial version.

   However, not all users who download these freemium apps go

with the in-app purchases. Some cannot be bothered and just delete the app. App developers, therefore, must design apps that are engaging enough to get users to take the IAP route.

2. **Advertisements.** This is one of the most common ways apps earn revenue. If you are a mobile user, you likely have experienced using a gaming app, for instance, and have seen ads while you wait for the game to load the next level. Basically, in-app advertisements are just like YouTube ads that earn when:

   - A user views an ad,
   - A user clicks on an ad, or
   - A user downloads the app you are advertising.

   Of course, the app earns less than a dollar for every ad view, click or download, so it is important that the app gets a lot of downloads to ensure there are enough users to see and interact with the ads.

3. **Subscriptions.** Subscription-based apps work just like regular newspaper and magazine subscriptions. Users download the app for free, which may or may not have some content. In order to unlock all the content in the app, the user pays a monthly or yearly subscription fee. For this kind of model to work, the app must regularly have fresh content that users love to consume, for example, interesting news, videos, make up tutorials, recipes, and the like.

4. **Affiliate marketing.** Apps earn affiliate income in the same way websites and YouTube videos earn from affiliate marketing. In a way, this method is similar to advertising. The app displays ads and earns when users view, click and install the app ad. But unlike in advertising (where the ad network decides which ads to show in the app), the app developer himself chooses the ads his app will earn from. This he does by signing up with an affiliate network, and choosing mobile app affiliate offers to integrate in his app.

5. **Email marketing.** This tried and tested method of marketing does not just work for websites; it works for apps too. Apps can collect

email addresses that can be used to hyper-target users that are most likely to buy a certain product or service. An app can unlock an additional feature in exchange for a user's email address. The app can also give free coins or likes in exchange for a Facebook or Twitter "like" or "follow," since doing so can also be used to collect email addresses through special software.

6. **App-related merchandise.** A very popular app can have additional income through physical merch. Take Rovio, for example. From a simple free game (the now - iconic Angry Birds), it has transformed itself to include products like clothing, accessories, toys and even movies, all in homage to the group of temperamental birds and their nemesis, the piggies.

Building Your Mobile Application

If all the details listed above sound exciting and interesting to you, then you would probably make a good app designer and earn a lot of income. Of course, it helps that you have a background in software engineering or computer science; the more you know, the better you will do at this business. However, your lack of skills and knowledge in these areas can be supplemented by training, or if you have really good business acumen, you can outsource to an app developer or designer who is willing to work and build an app for you.

Here is how you can start building your app development business from the ground up, as outlined by Carter Thomas of bluecloudsolutions.com;

1. **Write your business plan.** Again, a business plan will give you the direction that you need as you start building your business. You probably say you know what you are doing so there is no need for a plan. On the contrary, a plan will help you see better what you are doing, why you are doing it, and which resources you need to achieve your aims. Your business plan should also give you direction as to how fast you want to go, how many apps you want to develop and if you are doing this long term. Your business plan should also include your budget, without which you might end up with zero balance to your name. When you set your budget, make sure you stick to it.

2. **Do your homework.** As with any other endeavor and business, you need to know exactly what you are getting yourself into, especially the market you will penetrate. You probably have an idea about a new app, and you are most likely excited to put it out on the market because you think it will be the greatest app ever to hit the shelves. However, we need to pop your bubble. There are two million plus apps out there. What makes you think your app is original? Chances are, there is already an app that is similar to the one you are planning to create. Without doing your research, you might end up wasting time, money and effort putting together something that already exist, and is probably a lot better than yours.

   Instead of thinking about what you want for your app, you should be researching what the market wants. Survey the scene; what kinds of apps are making waves in the market right now? What do these apps do? How can you create something that is similarly popular and useful, and how can you differentiate your app from the competition? All these answers can be answered through comprehensive market research.

3. **Choose your app market.** Which platform will you be developing your app for? There are a number of markets, but it would be safe to go with the largest: the Apple App Store, Google Play or Amazon. Of course, it is possible to customize your app for many markets to improve the likelihood of getting more downloads. However, you need to learn about these markets to make an informed choice.

4. **Know the basics of programming languages.** The mention of programming is enough to make some people take a 180-degree turn and abandon their plans. But you do not really need to worry about this; you just need to know the difference between Java, Objective-C and HTML5 and what these coding languages are used for. You could do some reading to get a basic understanding of these languages, what kind of apps use these languages, and how much they cost.

5. **Decide on the app design.** This does not mean choosing which colors or font design your app will come in, although it would greatly help if you had a detailed idea of how you want the app to look and feel. App design refers to the features, integrations and other things you would include in the app. Do you want to have push notifications? Advertisements? Do you want it to connect to users' Facebook and Twitter accounts? You must take note of all these so you can communicate them to your app developer.

6. **Outsource to your app developer and designer.** If you are satisfied with the details of the app you are planning, then it is time to call in the pros, that is, if you are not going to develop and design the app yourself. The best way to find an app developer is to ask for recommendations from experts. You can also go to freelance outsourcing sites like Upwork. Make sure that you thoroughly screen the proposals you will get. Read feedback and reviews, ask for samples and see how well they can communicate with you. When you find the person, make sure you lay down everything in writing, the job scope, the fees, the deadlines and even the ownership of the app.

7. **Set up a developer account.** This account will help you publish the app and make it available to the public. You can start by signing up as an individual, and if you think you can make this big, you can upgrade to a business account. You need to share some of your login credentials with your developer and designer, since they will be the ones working directly on the app.

8. **Test your app and make the necessary changes.** Ask the developer to install app builds to your mobile and friends' mobiles so they can test the app. Gather as much feedback as you can, communicate these to your developer and commission them to make the revisions.

9. **Optimize the app for the platform you are uploading it to.** This means making the app visible through the app title, keywords, icons, description, category and rating. To hit this nail right on the head, you need to do your research. Make sure that your app stands out from the rest.

10. **Plan your marketing strategy.** Unless you can get users to download your app, you will not earn any income. Upload your app in the app store does not mean you will automatically get downloads. To get the word out about your new app, you need to use a variety of marketing strategies through social media, mobile ads, emails, videos and reviews, among others. You can also blog about the app and create a microsite in order to create excitement for the app's release.

11. **Launch your app.** Depending on the platform, your app will be included in the app list for downloads right away, or will be reviewed before it gets released. In order to make the process faster, you can upload your app to PreApps, an app marketplace for beta testers and lead users (which means you have to test your app again and get some more feedback and revise if you need to). When you have the app uploaded on the platform of your choice, you can start marketing using the strategies you have outlined in Step Ten.

CHAPTER 15:

Useful Links

"The best time to plant a tree was 20 years ago. The second best time is now."

- Chinese proverb.

Choosing a Product:

https://onthejoblearning.wordpress.com/2013/11/25/a-start-ups-litmus-test/

https://www.entrepreneurs-journey.com/8190/how-to-create-a-product/

http://www.iwillteachyoutoberich.com/blog/why-most-people-fail-at-making-online-products-and-how-you-can-win/

General Tips On Starting a Business

http://hackthesystem.com/blog/how-i-created-my-first-online-business/

Selling Information Products:

http://startupbros.com/9-ways-to-create-an-information-product-with-zero-expertise/

http://www.chrisg.com/selling-information-products/

http://www.forbes.com/sites/dorieclark/2014/02/10/how-to-create-and-sell-information-products/#1a1095b455ad

https://www.wakeupcloud.com/information-product-business/

https://econsultancy.com/blog/66247-14-examples-of-evergreen-content-formats-that-work-wonders/

http://contentmarketinginstitute.com/2014/12/how-to-curate-content/

https://www.ventureharbour.com/7-ways-to-sell-more-information-products/

https://theblogpress.com/blog/information-products-how-to-sell-a-beginners-guide/

http://www.hongkiat.com/blog/sell-ebooks/

https://www.entrepreneurs-journey.com/8190/how-to-create-a-product/

http://smallbusiness.chron.com/estimate-market-demand-using-adwords-32490.html

https://www.shopify.com/guides/what-to-sell/evaluating-market-demand

https://www.myecovermaker.com/blog/8-best-free-ebook-cover-design-tools/

http://www.artfulpublications.com/5-simple-tips-ebook-cover-design-success/

http://www.ecommercefuel.com/writing-product-descriptions/

https://www.smashwords.com/about/how_to_publish_on_smashwords

https://kdp.amazon.com/signin

https://sigil-ebook.com/

http://www.edudemic.com/most-popular-ebook-formats/

http://www.thecreativepenn.com/2014/10/10/read-your-own-audiobook/

http://blog.teachable.com/how-to-write-a-powerful-sales-page-with-joanna-wiebe

http://femaleentrepreneurassociation.com/2014/08/4-steps-to-writing-an-amazing-sales-page-that-converts/

http://www.copyblogger.com/successful-sales-pages/

https://founderu.selz.com/

http://www.hongkiat.com/blog/sell-ebooks/

https://alexisgrant.com/2015/04/22/self-publishing-sell-your-ebook-on-amazon/

https://janefriedman.com/10-questions-epublishing/

http://fitsmallbusiness.com/how-to-create-a-business-facebook-page/#comments

https://blog.hubspot.com/blog/tabid/6307/bid/28441/
The-15-Best-Facebook-Pages-You-ve-Ever-Seen.
aspx#sm.000002r0wb1p7lczvr02t8xzk846m

http://www.wordstream.com/blog/ws/2015/09/14/facebook-advertising-cost

https://adespresso.com/academy/guides/facebook-ads-beginner/

http://www.socialmediaexaminer.com/9-ways-to-use-facebook-groups-for-business/

http://www.postplanner.com/use-facebook-groups-for-marketing-business/

http://neilpatel.com/what-is-google-adwords/

https://econsultancy.com/blog/65682-what-is-google-adwords-and-how-does-it-work/

Selling Through Affiliates:

http://www.sparkplugging.com/affiliate-business-online/

http://realpassiveincomeideas.com/blogs-advertising-affiliate-marketing-examples/

https://www.authorityhacker.com/successful-affiliate-websites-examples/

https://www.bloggertipstricks.com/find-affiliate-products.html

https://www.bloggertipstricks.com/affiliate-marketing-keyword-research.html

https://alexisgrant.com/2015/02/10/affiliate-sales-guide/

http://www.buyqualityplr.com/list-of-profitable-evergreen-niches/

https://designshack.net/articles/business-articles/free-websites-who-has-them-and-which-you-should-use/

http://thegrue.org/how-free-web-hosting-works-and-why-to-avoid-it/

https://makeawebsitehub.com/affiliate-marketing-networks/

http://www.highpayingaffiliateprograms.com/affiliate-network/

https://www.authorityhacker.com/how-to-make-money-from-clickbank/

Online Training Courses:

http://www.forbes.com/sites/dorieclark/2014/08/06/how-to-create-a-money-making-online-course/#3529128d4e3e

https://socialtriggers.com/online-courses-create-and-sell/

http://www.incomediary.com/make-money-with-udemy

http://www.skilledup.com/articles/online-education-vs-traditional-education-the-pros-and-cons

https://potomac.edu/learning/online-learning-vs-traditional-learning/

https://www.academyofmine.com/70-ideas-for-online-courses/

https://www.techsmith.com/camtasia.html

http://www.capterra.com/course-authoring-software/

http://www.learningrevolution.net/sell-online-courses/

http://www.slideshare.net/RobCubbon/16-tips-on-how-to-make-money-on-udemy-passive-income-from-teaching-online/12-Your_rst_video_course_will

http://www.ivetriedthat.com/2013/03/18/how-to-create-and-make-money-from-your-own-online-course/

http://www.incomediary.com/make-money-with-udemy

http://www.slideshare.net/RobCubbon/16-tips-on-how-to-make-money-on-udemy-passive-income-from-teaching-online/78-If_youre_interested_in_earningpassive

Blogging:

https://www.authorityhacker.com/make-money-blogging/

http://www.bloggingwizard.com/drive-more-traffic-to-your-blog/

http://www.vervesearch.com/blog/5-powerful-tactics-to-increase-your-blog-traffic/

https://blog.kissmetrics.com/double-your-social-media-traffic/

https://www.americanexpress.com/us/small-business/openforum/articles/20-ways-to-drive-more-traffic-to-your-blog/

http://roadtoblogging.com/adsense-alternatives/

https://www.nutsandboltsmedia.com/how-does-adsense-work/

http://powerpinoys.com/earn-money-blogging-philippines/

https://allbloggingtips.com/godaddy-alternatives/

http://www.wpbeginner.com/showcase/wordpress-competitors-23-popular-alternatives-to-wordpress/

http://www.doughroller.net/make-money/list-of-personal-finance-blogs-that-have-sold-for-1-million-or-more/

https://www.quora.com/What-do-I-write-my-first-blog-post-on

http://www.forbes.com/sites/johnrampton/2016/03/23/a-guide-to-how-often-and-when-to-post-content/#5dee36904616

Making YouTube videos:

http://fortunelords.com/youtube-statistics/

http://www.businessinsider.com/popular-kid-youtube-stars-2016-6/#fulltimekid-with-mya-is-a-channel-for-kids-to-learn-to-do-experiments-and-crafts-from-a-peer-2

https://www.youtube.com/user/TheYoungTurks

https://www.linkedin.com/in/steven-oh-8a87a25

https://www.youtube.com/watch?v=iuqfQ4Quwp4

http://www.tubefilter.com/2014/02/03/youtube-average-cpm-advertising-rate/

https://www.quora.com/How-much-money-can-I-make-from-a-YouTube-video-with-5-000-views

https://www.quora.com/How-much-does-a-YouTuber-with-1-million-subscribers-earn-in-a-year/answer/Chhaya-Sharma-24?srid=uJK3a&share=421e0819

https://support.google.com/youtube/answer/2467968?hl=en

https://support.google.com/adwords/answer/2375464?hl=en

https://www.techwalla.com/articles/definitions-of-cpm-cpv-cpc

https://support.google.com/youtube/topic/1115890?hl=en&ref_topic=1115889

http://www.vlognation.com/earn-money-youtube-sponsorships/

https://www.youtube.com/watch?v=xEx4uYiBa3g

https://www.youtube.com/watch?v=mUx7IR3_oQo

https://support.google.com/youtube/answer/154235?hl=en

https://grin.co/youtube-sponsorship-for-small-channels/

Being an Outsourcer:

http://searchcio.techtarget.com/definition/outsourcing

http://www.chrisducker.com/how-outsourcing-works/

https://www.fespa.com/news/features/why-is-outsourcing-a-good-business-strategy.html

http://ezinearticles.com/?Why-Moms-Go-Freelance&id=787572

http://ezinearticles.com/?Why-Hire-a-Freelancer-for-Your-Project?&id=7112298

http://ezinearticles.com/?Freelancing-and-Why-Use-a-Freelancer?&id=5758452

https://www.freshbooks.com/blog/freelance-jobs

https://www.thebalance.com/take-advantage-of-other-companies-outsourcing-needs-393520

http://www.incomediary.com/outsourcing-work-on-the-internet

http://www.incomediary.com/10-steps-to-successful-outsourcing

http://www.proz.com/forum/getting_established/129286-about_becoming_an_outsourcer.html

https://www.gov.uk/paye-for-employers/paye-and-payroll

https://www.gov.uk/working-for-yourself

http://www.webdesignerdepot.com/2010/04/20-reasons-you-shouldnt-be-a-freelancer/

http://yourfreelanceguy.blogspot.com/2011/06/what-is-freelancer.html

http://millo.co/takes-freelance-full-time

http://www.myoddjobs.co.uk/

Freelance Writing:

http://ezinearticles.com/?How-Do-I-Become-a-Freelance-Writer-If-I-Have-No-Online-Writing-Experience?&id=2270201

http://www.frontierwriters.com/working-as-a-freelance-writer-some-common-pros-and-cons.php

 http://writinghouse.org/blog/100-reasons-to-become-a-freelance-writer/

https://www.writersincharge.com/freelance-writing-fail/

http://www.huffingtonpost.com/sherry-gray/you-really-can-make-a-liv_b_9393902.html

http://www.freelancewritinggigs.com/2008/12/30-types-of-freelance-writing-jobs-and-how-to-get-them/

https://www.onespace.com/blog/2015/10/6-types-of-freelance-writer/

http://have-a-word.com/15-types-of-freelance-writing-jobs/

https://www.thebalance.com/guide-to-freelancing-1794537

http://www.businessinsider.com/how-to-start-freelance-writing-2016-4

http://www.makealivingwriting.com/

http://www.makealivingwriting.com/websites-that-pay-writers-2015-79-sites/

https://thewritelife.com/find-freelance-writing-jobs/

https://elnacain.com/find-freelance-writing-jobs/

http://menwithpens.ca/three-scams-freelancers-face-and-how-to-avoid-them/

http://freelanceflyer.com/wp-content/uploads/2014/03/10-Unexpected-Places-to-Find-Freelance-Writing-Clients-Freelance-Flyer.pdf

Becoming a Web Consultant:

http://www.consultingsuccess.com/web-consulting-an-introduction

http://www.consultingsuccess.com/web-design-consulting-essentials

http://www.mlwebco.com/2009/11/12/more-than-a-web-designer-a-web-consultant/#comment-977714

http://www.wisegeek.com/what-is-a-web-consultant.htm

https://www.freshconsulting.com/websites/ http://simondelasalle.com/expertise/web-consultant/

http://www.protofuse.com/blog/website-consultant-35-ways-improve-website/

http://work.chron.com/become-website-consultant-14693.html

https://www.jimdo.com/2015/01/23/7-tips-to-build-a-great-consultants-website/

http://www.vandelaydesign.com/become-a-consultant/

http://www.wisegeek.net/how-do-i-become-a-web-consultant.htm

http://www.executionists.com/much-website-cost-2016/

Being an Internet Marketing Consultant:

http://ezinearticles.com/?Can-You-Become-a-Professional-Internet-Marketing-Consultant?&id=120410

https://www.entrepreneur.com/businessideas/internet-marketing-consultant

http://ezinearticles.com/?What-Does-a-Local-Internet-Marketing-Consultant-Do?&id=5797867

http://www.studententerprise.ie/phases/phase-2/module4/what-is-market-research/

https://www.business.tas.gov.au/growing-and-improving-your-business/marketing-your-business/preparing-a-marketing-plan[

https://moz.com/beginners-guide-to-seo

http://www.skyword.com/contentstandard/marketing/email-marketing-strategy-why-you-should-treat-your-newsletter-like-its-own-publishing-destination/

http://www.marketing-schools.org/types-of-marketing/viral-marketing.html

http://www.socialmediaexaminer.com/10-successful-facebook-marketing-examples/

http://www.copyblogger.com/pinterest-marketing/

http://coschedule.com/blog/how-to-use-pinterest-for-marketing/

https://blog.bufferapp.com/pinterest-marketing-tips

http://www.cio.com/article/2380667/twitter/14-ways-to-use-twitter-to-market-your-business.html

http://www.digitalmarketer.com/

http://www.wikihow.com/Be-an-Internet-Marketer

https://valuecreationprofit.com/how-to-become-an-online-internet-marketer

http://www.clickbank.com/tips-to-becoming-a-successful-internet-marketer/

http://www.usanfranonline.com/resources/internet-marketing/5-traits-of-a-great-internet-marketer/

Amazon E-book Publishing:

https://www.theguardian.com/books/booksblog/2016/mar/21/for-me-traditional-publishing-means-poverty-but-self-publish-no-way

http://www.forbes.com/sites/jaymcgregor/2015/04/17/mark-dawson-made-750000-from-self-published-amazon-books/#9efe18d35e38

http://thoughtcatalog.com/cody-delistraty/2013/09/21-harsh-but-eye-opening-writing-tips-from-great-authors/

http://www.therichest.com/celebnetworth/celeb/authors/stephenie-meyer-net-worth/

https://www.contentbistro.com/2016/05/26/42-easy-and-effortless-ebook-ideas-for-the-time-starved-entrepreneur/

http://blog.osmosio.com/ebook-ideas-for-any-niche/

http://www.bigbrandsystem.com/11-coolest-ebook-ideas-ever/

http://www.sfwa.org/2009/06/7-reasons-fiction-writers-should-sell-nonfiction/

http://thewritepractice.com/nonfiction-vs-fiction/

http://www.salon.com/2013/03/15/hey_amazon_wheres_my_money/

http://thoughtcatalog.com/cody-delistraty/2013/09/21-harsh-but-eye-opening-writing-tips-from-great-authors/

http://www.writersdigest.com/online-editor/8-ways-to-prepare-to-write-your-nonfiction-book-in-a-month

https://kdp.amazon.com/help?topicId=A3288N75MH14B8

https://kdp.amazon.com/help?topicId=A37Z49E2DDQPP3&ref_=gs

http://www.thecreativepenn.com/2014/08/30/exclusivity/

http://badredheadmedia.com/2015/08/30/which-is-right-for-you-a-quick-guide-to-kdp-vs-kdp-select/

http://www.acx.com/

https://www.createspace.com/services?utm_id=4476&smk=Help_Section&ref=365810&ls=Amazon&sls=Author_Central&cp=70170000000Ac75&rewrite=true

https://kdp.amazon.com/help?topicId=A37Z49E2DDQPP3&ref_=gs

http://www.copyblogger.com/how-to-publish-kindle-ebook/

https://adespresso.com/academy/blog/5-must-do-ways-market-free-ebook/

http://www.huffingtonpost.com/fauzia-burke/ways-to-promote-your-ebook_b_3963836.html

http://contentmarketinginstitute.com/2016/02/promote-your-ebook/

http://www.thecreativepenn.com/2014/04/22/promote-first-book/

Mobile Marketing:

http://marketingland.com/forecast-half-of-consumers-will-be-paying-with-phones-by-2018-158609

http://www.gartner.com/newsroom/id/3178217

https://smallbiztrends.com/2016/11/mobile-marketing-trends-for-2017.html

https://www.impactbnd.com/blog/mobile-marketing-statistics-for-2016

https://blog.unitag.io/bonus-emails/defining-qr-codes-and-mobile-marketing/

http://www.wordstream.com/blog/ws/2013/08/19/what-is-mobile-marketing

http://fatguymedia.com/what-is-mobile-marketing/

https://www.mmaglobal.co.uk/how-effective-is-mobile-marketing.html

https://www.brandingstrategyinsider.com/2016/09/ten-characteristics-of-the-modern-marketer.html#.WIYtFaJ97Eb

http://www.knowthis.com/what-is-marketing/characteristics-of-modern-marketers

http://sethgodin.typepad.com/all_marketers_are_liars/2012/10/not-liars-storytellers.html

http://www.telegraph.co.uk/connect/media-and-technology/ten-qualities-modern-marketers-must-have/

http://www.business2community.com/mobile-apps/can-mobile-marketers-expect-peers-2017-01681381#gaBA6wJcBXh8Bf4T.97

https://www.entrepreneur.com/article/287024

http://www.forbes.com/sites/jaysondemers/2016/11/10/7-social-media-marketing-trends-that-will-dominate-2017/#4ef338073a28

http://www.smartinsights.com/managing-digital-marketing/marketing-innovation/digital-marketing-trends-2016-2017/

http://www.wikihow.com/Become-a-Mobile-Marketing-Consultant

http://digitaldeepak.com/digital-marketing-expert/#

http://www.forbes.com/sites/allbusiness/2016/03/16/launch-your-future-consulting-career-in-6-steps-before-quitting-your-day-job/print/

Local Business Consulting:

https://www.gov.uk/set-up-business

http://www.learnhowtobecome.org/consultant/

https://www.entrepreneur.com/article/41384

http://www.passionforbusiness.com/articles/be-a-small-business-consultant.htm

https://karmicconsulting.net/2013/08/how-i-got-17345-new-visitors-one-cease-and-desist-letter-and-a-10-fold-increase-in-new-client-calls-with-100-free-traffic-and-so-too-can-you/

http://ezinearticles.com/?Local-Business-Marketing-Brings-More-Income&id=5260503

http://study.com/articles/What_Does_a_Consultant_Do.html

https://www.quicksprout.com/2011/09/19/7-lessons-learned-from-running-a-consulting-company/

http://www.bizfilings.com/Libraries/pdfs/starting-consulting-business-guide.sflb.ashx

http://articles.bplans.com/so-you-want-to-start-consulting-part-1/

http://www.forbes.com/sites/dailymuse/2013/11/05/be-the-best-consultant-ever-6-things-that-will-make-you-great/#11a420c72996

http://ezinearticles.com/?Start-a-Local-Community-Consulting-Business-(-and-7-Easy-Offers-You-Can-Launch-For-for-Under-$100)&id=7977677

Becoming an App Designer:

http://www.techradar.com/news/phone-and-communications/
mobile-phones/what-are-apps-and-how-do-they-work-with-your-
smartphone-1141429

http://www.digitaltrends.com/mobile/android-app-stores/

https://www.smashingmagazine.com/2015/04/thinking-like-an-app-
designer/

http://mashable.com/2012/08/27/app-developer-
infographic/#U3S2VAco4sqg

http://www.smartappmarketer.com/how-do-free-apps-make-money/

http://www.forbes.com/sites/tristanlouis/2013/08/10/how-much-do-
average-apps-make/#2e45dcdc12cb

https://fueled.com/blog/much-money-can-earn-app/

http://www.optimisedtech.com/2014/06/top-reasons-on-why-mobile-
apps-are.html

http://blush.digital/blog/why-are-mobile-apps-so-popular

https://tappublisher.com/blog/why-mobile-apps-are-so-popular/26

http://www.techradar.com/news/phone-and-communications/
mobile-phones/what-are-apps-and-how-do-they-work-with-your-
smartphone-1141429

https://techcrunch.com/2015/06/02/6-1b-smartphone-users-globally-
by-2020-overtaking-basic-fixed-phone-subscriptions/

http://www.cio.com/article/3064234/small-business/7-ways-small-
businesses-can-benefit-from-mobile-apps.html

http://www.forbes.com/sites/allbusiness/2014/11/17/heres-why-your-
business-needs-its-own-mobile-app/#780451845c76

https://savvyapps.com/blog/how-do-free-apps-make-money

https://www.biznessapps.com/blog/5-ways-mobile-apps-can-help-you-
grow-your-business/

https://buildfire.com/ways-business-benefit-having-mobile-app/

https://www.appboy.com/blog/in-app-purchase-stats/

https://www.lifewire.com/how-to-make-money-by-selling-free-apps-2373430

https://www.allbusiness.com/12-step-guide-to-building-your-first-mobile-app-11193-1.html/5

CHAPTER 16:

INSPIRING

"Do not wait; the time will never be 'just right.' Start where you stand, and work with whatever tools you may have at your command, and better tools will be found as you go along."

- George Herbert

"Change your life today. Don't gamble on the future, act now, without delay."

– Simone de Beauvoir

"I can accept failure, everyone fails at something. But I can't accept not trying."

– Michael Jordan

"It does not matter how slowly you go as long as you do not stop."

– Confucius

"Excellence is not a singular act, but a habit. You are what you repeatedly do"

– Shaquille O'Neal

"If you accept the expectations of others, especially negative ones, then you never will change the outcome."

– Michael Jordan

Vision is perhaps our greatest strength... it has kept us alive to the power and continuity of thought through the centuries, it makes us peer into the future and lends shape to the unknown.

– Li Ka-shing

"Always do your best. What you plant now, you will harvest later."

– Og Mandino

"Start where you are. Use what you have. Do what you can."

– Arthur Ashe

"Life is 10% what happens to you and 90% how you react to it."

– Charles R. Swindoll

"The secret of getting ahead is getting started."

- Mark Twain

"Believe in yourself! Have faith in your abilities! Without a humble but reasonable confidence in your own powers you cannot be successful or happy."

– Norman Vincent Peale

"Do the difficult things while they are easy and do the great things while they are small. A journey of a thousand miles must begin with a single step."

– Lao Tzu

"One of the things is we tend to give up too soon. We get knocked down a couple of times, and we stay down. It's so important to get back up again."

– Og Mandino

"Sometimes, things may not go your way, but the effort should be there every single night."

– Michael Jordan

Resources to help you start, grow and profit from your own home business

https://homebusinesses4all.com/resoures

Did you like this book? Please recommend us to a friend here:

https://homebusinesses4all.com/bookoffer

Free Training on how to create and sell an online course:

https://homebusinesses4all.com/ignite

Do you want a Mentor to take you to 10K per month and beyond? Read more about how you can have one on one help and support to help you create your ideal online business to support the lifestyle you desire

https://homebusinesses4all.com/elite

Printed in Great Britain
by Amazon

38424578R00097